STATE OF
MIND

STATE OF MIND
Politics, Uncertainty and the
Search for the Jamaican Dream

Chris Tufton

IAN RANDLE PUBLISHERS
Kingston • Miami

First published in Jamaica, 2019 by
Ian Randle Publishers
16 Herb McKenley Drive
Box 686
Kingston 6
www.ianrandlepublishers.com

© 2019, Christopher Tufton
ISBN: 978-976-637-974-2 (pbk)
        978-976-637-990-2 (hbk)

National Library of Jamaica Cataloguing in Publication Data

Tufton, Christopher
    State of mind : politics, uncertainty and the search for the Jamaican
dream / Christopher Tufton.

    p. ; cm.

    ISBN 978-976-637-974-2 (pbk)

1. Tufton, Christopher, 1968 – Biography
2. Jamaica – Biography
3. Politicians – Jamaica – Biography
4. Jamaica – Politics and government
I. Title

920   dc 23

Published with the support of The CHASE Fund.

Front cover art by Nicholas Anglin
Cover design by Jaime Grandison
Author photo by Tiffany Lue-Yen

Book design by Ian Randle Publishers
Printed in United States of America

In tribute to my mother, Ruby.
And to my alma mater, Manchester High School.
*The two most powerful influences on my life and
the person I have become.*

CONTENTS

FOREWORD

As students of political science we contend with the forces that shape democracy, governance and political culture, and with the ensuing outcomes. As abstract and theoretical as they might be, it is critical to understand them and how they work in order to understand and predict how politics and policy shape our society and, by extension, our individual lives.

In telling the story of his political journey from his teenage years to his present position as a member of Cabinet – with all the details of the turbulence along the way – Chris Tufton does something that we seldom witness in Jamaica and the Caribbean: he gives an honest and grounded account of firsthand experience in competitive party politics and in democratic governance. In so doing, Tufton provides us with the means to take a significant step forward in truly understanding Jamaican democracy and political culture.

The main thrust of Tufton's memoir is his experience in Jamaican party politics. From his political formation in high school, to his joining Young Jamaica at UWI, Mona, he proceeds to share a detailed account of his involvement with the National Democratic Movement (NDM), Jamaica's most successful third party since independence. This telling of the NDM story alone sets the book apart as, to date, we have not had a reasoned, informed account of the party's formation and trajectory, and the sea change it brought to Jamaican political culture, democracy, and governance. Tufton does this comprehensively and brings to the fore cogent points about the NDM's ongoing legacy.

Tufton also makes a seminal contribution to the literature on the Jamaica Labour Party (JLP). Most of what has been written about the JLP, whether in academia or other books and articles, has been biased, incomplete, and simplistic. Tufton does his part to rectify that imbalance with a nuanced and reflective insider account of the period 2002–2016. He also does something in this book that is far too seldom done by going through the on-the-ground activities and work that are done in representing a constituency and in holding a position as a cabinet minister.

Throughout his telling of the details and dynamics of the nitty-gritty of competitive politics, both between the JLP and the People's National Party (PNP) and within the JLP, Tufton candidly shares aspects of his own life. From the outside, Tufton's story may seem fairly unremarkable, and in many ways he does have a lot in common with the many other fatherless Jamaicans who have risen from their original modest circumstances to positions of prominence and success through education, ambition, and hard work. Throughout his recounting, however, he grapples with the role of the church, race and colour, migration, and other controversial issues, and brings to these topics original and nuanced perspectives that add to – and are likely to complicate – these conversations.

Perhaps the most important contribution that Tufton makes in this book, however, is towards a better and clearer understanding of the deficiencies of Jamaica's political culture, in particular the paternalism that precludes the effective use of time and resources, and which keeps Jamaica from moving forward as it ought to.

Democracy is about civic engagement, it is about deliberation and inclusiveness, it is about fostering spaces of interconnected dialogue between not just politics but between all that which concerns social life. *State of Mind* brings these ideas to life in an accessible and interesting way.

This book signals a new kind of political thought in the region and will undoubtedly become part of Jamaica's political canon. It is a book that all Jamaicans – and anyone who wants to understand Jamaica's politics – should read.

Dr Lloyd Waller
Head, Department of Government
University of the West Indies
Mona Campus
Jamaica

Acknowledgements

The CHASE Fund provided significant financial support for the writing, editing and publication of this book.

My sister Sharon Miller read an early version of the book and corrected family details, and together with my Aunt Annette, she reminded me of other family stories that enriched that section of the book immensely.

Delroy Hunter has been my friend from Chancellor Hall, and has been there for me throughout; I could not have written this book without his support and counsel. My cousin and friend Din Duggan gave ongoing feedback and encouragement.

I was honoured that the writer and poet Dr Ralph Thompson, despite ill health, read the entire manuscript and gave valuable comments, which boosted my confidence in the project and helped keep me going.

Professor Tony Harriott's close reading of the manuscript, and his discerning insight, caused me to reflect more on, and bring a deeper level of thought to, the events I have recounted in the book.

I am grateful to the Head of the UWI Mona Department of Government, Dr Lloyd Waller, for reading the book and writing a thoughtful and trenchant foreword.

And thanks to Diana Thorburn who believed in the book from the start, and assisted me through to its publication.

INTRODUCTION:
Why This Book

This is the story of how I came to be the person I am today, and how I see Jamaica and my role in its development. I don't think of this book as a memoir, but it is autobiographical. It is a personal story, and there are parts of it that I struggled to share publicly.

I was not born into a storybook world. My past was not painful, nor is there anything I am ashamed of. As a public figure for the past 20 years there are bits and pieces already out there. But putting my story down in its entirety, as I have in this book, does leave me feeling somewhat exposed and a bit vulnerable. Also my story is not mine alone, and I have had to weigh carefully how much I share so as not to intrude on the privacy of my friends and family, whose trust I would not want to violate.

But ultimately, I feel that I have offered myself to be a servant of the people whether I am actively involved in national politics or not. I would like to share with them – with you – who I am and how I got here.

I am an ordinary Jamaican from humble beginnings, but I have had the extraordinary opportunity and honour to see Jamaica from many different perspectives and to hold public office, and it is my calling to continue to serve Jamaica in whatever capacity I can.

Because of my work as an academic and university lecturer, I am aware of the importance of history and the need to set the record straight. Jamaica suffers a dearth of books on its politics, particularly books that are accessible outside of the academic elite, books which are relevant to all Jamaicans.

Moreover, the recording of Jamaican political history that does exist has been dominated by a particular, some might say, outdated, ideological view. Furthermore, it is much more favourable to the People's National Party (PNP) than it is to the Jamaica Labour Party (JLP), a slant that I don't agree is historically accurate. I hope, with this book, to provide a more objective account of what happened, how, and why, for students of Jamaican politics, and for the historical record.

There are also few 'insider' accounts of Jamaican politics. We read the newspapers, we listen to talk radio, we discuss politics among ourselves, but there is a lot of speculation, in part because we don't have the firsthand accounts from the players themselves. I personally enjoy reading the memoirs and personal stories of US and UK politicians who publish dozens of such books each year – it is almost par for the course in those countries that once you hold public office or have been involved in political life, even for a short time, that you write a book about it. We all learn from these books – whether we are curious about the inner workings of politics, or are just interested in the process.

Finally, I want to put on the record some of my thoughts about and my own vision for Jamaica. I have many ideas about how we can make Jamaica a better place, ideas born of my experiences thus far, together with my lifelong ambition to serve Jamaica. This book provides a vehicle for me to work through my thoughts and share these ideas with a wider public.

As this book goes to press, I am 50 years old, with – I hope, and with God's blessing – a lot of life left to live, a lot of work still to do, and a lot of goals still to attain. There is a quote often attributed to Buddha, 'the mind is everything; you become what you think.' Regardless of who came up with that, I ascribe to such a mindset.

I hope that you will read my story, and come away with a better understanding not only of my own journey, but also of Jamaica's journey, the role that each of us plays in Jamaica's development, and the power of each of us, harnessing our mind and our will and pursuing our goals without letting obstacles get in our way, to improve our own lives and the state of our country.

PROLOGUE

There is nothing entirely within our own power but our own thoughts.
Rene Descartes.

One of my earliest memories is of the time I was invited to join a gang when I was in the fourth grade. It was the age where I was starting to understand the world around me better, and things that I wasn't conscious of before were becoming more noticeable to me. One of the more popular youths in the school came up to me one day and asked if I wanted to be in his gang; I asked him what the gang did. 'Just control the school and beat up girls,' was his reply.

I declined the invitation, but I could just as easily have said yes. What made that incident even more unforgettable to me is that I saw that same fellow years later, and he had indeed become a real gangster. Could that have been me too? The thought crosses my mind from time to time. As a nine-year-old country boy, I knew very little about gangs. Perhaps it was a subconscious morality from so many Sundays in church that tipped me to say no? Some sense of right and wrong that even at such a young age I had an innate notion of? What made me different from the other boys who did join the gang? As much as one is a product of their home environment, chance can also play a role in the direction in which one's life goes. I turned him down, but at that young age how much of that I can attribute to good sense on my part, and how much to luck that I gave the 'right' answer at the time, I can only hazard a guess.

I reflect on this incident as I think about where I'm coming from and how I got to where I am. As I look back, this incident happened as I was coming to the understanding – inchoate and subconscious to begin with – that my life's path, while often determined by fate and by the circumstances of my birth and upbringing – the things I had no control over – was also largely determined by my own choices, will, effort, and determination. Whether it was to achieve a particular goal, or realize a certain outcome, or to fulfil a calling, I have largely made decisions about my life and its direction and then followed them through by my own relentless pursuit of my objectives. There have been many obstacles to my ambitions, but I have been blessed with the ability to recognize that in pursuing any goal there is only one way: forward.

After over 20 years in politics, I can see clearly how these three elements – my destiny, background, and outlook – have come together to shape my path. But of all these, it has been my own mindset that has determined how I have responded to how things have played out, and ultimately to the outcome of any situation.

This is the story I want to share.

A Jamaican Story

On the day I was born, January 21, 1968, a fatherless child to a single, working-class mother in Mandeville, Manchester, no one looking on from the outside could have – or would have – ever imagined that I would not only graduate from university, but would also earn a doctorate. That I would become a senator, a member of parliament, and a government minister would have been the furthest notions from most people's minds.

But I was born in a newly independent Jamaica when upward mobility through education and access to opportunities were more of a reality for children from working-class homes. I came of age in a period where Jamaica, too, was coming of age, defining its own identity, for itself and in the wider world, and my witness to that process helped to define my own sense of who I was, what I felt I was born to do, and the choices I have made – and continue to make – on my own journey.

My birth, 'out of wedlock', is not unusual in Jamaica – not when I was born in the late 1960s, nor today, where 85 per cent of children are born to unmarried mothers. My older sister, Sharon, was born to my mother when she was just a teenager, and we were later joined by Brian in 1972. My father was not around, nor were theirs. My mother went on to marry a church brother, Ronald Blake, in the late '70s, and then Shelly and Andrew joined our family.

The fact that my siblings and I all thrived in every regard – socially, academically, and professionally – can be attributed to the stability that we enjoyed as children. Like many other Jamaican children born to single mothers, we belie the claim that children born to and raised by single mothers are more likely to commit crimes and are less likely to complete their education, among other negative outcomes. Research has shown that in Jamaica and the English-speaking Caribbean, and my personal experience bears out, that it is not family structure that is important – it does not matter if it is a single-parent household or if there are children by different fathers – what matters most is family stability. When a child is shifted from one household to another, he does not have the solid foundation he needs to thrive. The child who does not have an adult consistently looking out for his best interests – whether that adult is a parent, relative, or otherwise – is the child who will develop problems in life.

Indeed, I was fortunate to enjoy the benefits of what one might call the 'flip side' of being born to a single mother. During my early years, I was raised by her extended family in a large family compound in Battersea, Mandeville. My maternal grandmother, Henrietta Charlton, was my primary caregiver, with support from my grandfather Uriah Spencer – known as Mass Pun – and many aunts and uncles. And then there were more relatives and neighbours who, even when there was no blood relation, performed the roles of family members.

In effect, I was raised by the village. There was a sense of responsibility among ourselves; we were each other's brother's keeper, as it were. Children moved from one yard to another, and could always be sure they would receive a meal wherever they went. I remember my grandmother forgoing her own dinner in order for a visiting child to eat.

It was a working-class community. My mother was the eighth of eleven children. My grandparents, both originally from Hanbury District and Bonitto Crescent in Mandeville, were from humble backgrounds. My grandfather was a mason and backyard farmer and sometimes a truck driver. My grandmother was a housewife in the first few decades of their marriage, but later worked as a household helper to supplement the family's income. My aunts and uncles were employed as plumbers, office helpers, secretaries, and office administrators; there was a minister of religion and a lab technician.

I may not have had a father or an ideal two-parent home, but I had everything I needed to succeed. I attended pre-school and then primary school. Perhaps one of the factors auguring for my eventual success was that my Aunt Annette worked at the Manchester Parish Library and always ensured I had books to read, and that I read them.

And I had a lot of love.

I am far from unique in this regard – mine is the story of many Jamaicans born to similar types of families, who have defied the conventional wisdom, the dire predictions, and the pundits' so-called wisdom and gone on to stable, productive lives.

Looking back now, it seems almost impossible that I could have grown up so carefree and happy, that perhaps my memories of such an innocent and idyllic childhood could possibly be skewed. But I attribute those years to having laid the foundation of who I am today: positive, optimistic, and confident that things will somehow work out, no matter how adverse the circumstances might appear. And that has to have come from a place much like the treasured home of my childhood memory.

When I was very young, my mother lived in Ensom City, Spanish Town, working in Kingston as a Labour Officer. Though we lived apart, she visited regularly, and I was so well cared for by my grandparents and extended family that I have no memory of missing her as one might expect a child would miss his mother. My bonds to both my mother and my extended family were solid.

When I was six, I went to live with my mother for about two years, and attended the Crescent Primary School. I then returned to my grandmother until Mummy moved back to Mandeville when I was nine, and we all – I, my siblings, and later her new husband – established a home together in Greenvale.

But even amid this rosy scenario, there were some aspects of family life that were not all positive: my mother's marriage ended in divorce after seven years. While she was married, my stepfather was not much of a father figure as he still worked in Kingston and was only around on some weekends. My mother was the primary breadwinner and, once we were all under her roof, virtually raised us as a single parent, despite the marriage.

In the Jamaican scheme of things, we would have been working class. Once my mother established herself in the workforce and bought her own home, we would probably have been re-classified as lower middle class. It is only in retrospect that I see these things; at the time they were of no import. While we were certainly not well-off, we never lacked for anything, and I never felt deprived. It was only when I reached high school that I began to notice that some students were materially better off than I was, that some children were driven to school in cars, while I walked or took route taxis.

My world was certainly not perfect; I can see that now, but it seemed perfect to me then. Even in retrospect I have only fond, happy childhood memories, and I am grateful for this having been the world in which I got my start.

Ole' Time Religion

Like many Jamaican children, I grew up in the church. My mother was a devout Christian and going to church on Sundays – and often on weekdays – was one of our most important activities; as important as school.

We attended United Brethren of Christ, an evangelical denomination that came to Jamaica in 1944 as the US base of the church sought to expand its mission overseas. Church services, functions, and prayer meetings were at the centre of our calendar; everything else was scheduled around them. We lived within walking distance, so it was easy to go to and from. Friday nights were youth nights – drama, sports and games, all with a Christian theme or focus. I went to Sunday school and sang in a church quartet for many years. I liked girls a lot, and if I followed my instincts…well, church helped to keep me from not getting into too much trouble in my teenage years.

Ours was a traditional, conservative church, and Mummy was a dedicated member. She sought to live as the church prescribed, and didn't even like my sisters to wear pants, or for us to go to the movies. We prayed at mealtimes, we had devotions at home, and we hosted prayer meetings at our house. My aunts were also deeply involved in the church.

As is customary in many Jamaican fundamentalist Christian churches, I was baptized at 12 years old, when I was considered old enough to accept the Lord as my saviour. In preparation for this, I studied the scriptures intensively, and got even more involved in the church's activities. It was my decision, I worked towards it, and I was eager to mark this rite of passage.

While I would never claim to be a model of pious Christian virtue, then or now, my formative years in the church have left indelible marks on my outlook, my behaviour, my attitudes, and my understanding of the meaning of life, though this is always evolving. Between what I learned in church and what my mother emphasized at home, my grounding is typical of the conservative Jamaican with regard to what are called 'family values' – the traditional if illusory (in Jamaica) heterosexual nuclear family model, and the corollary attitudes that come with that.

As I have matured, I have come to have a much more informed and nuanced view of the church, particularly as a social and political institution. I have a less naïve awareness of the reality of the Jamaican society that I am a part of, and I recognize that the passion and force with which many Jamaicans defend 'family values' is at odds with our behaviour, not only in terms of promiscuity and infidelity but also with regard to the callous disregard that so many Jamaicans seem to have for the value of human life.

I see the church as a source of moral teaching and of personal spiritual fulfilment, but I recognize the critical roles that the church plays in a country like Jamaica, some of which can be paradoxical and even problematic. There is no questioning the role that Christian churches in Jamaica have played in the education system, as providers of social services in areas that the state has not been able to look after, for one reason or another, and as much-needed stable societal institutions.

But there is a debate to be had that while the church may be a source of spiritual fulfilment and refuge for many people, it might also be a convenient mechanism by which people absolve themselves of responsibility in working through challenging situations as they 'leave it in God's hands'. For someone like myself who believes in dealing with adverse situations by facing them directly and figuring out how to move past the adversity and proceed forward, I personally have a difficulty with this worldview.

There are too many church-going people in Jamaica who accept a less-than-ideal situation, whether it is in their domestic life, their work, or their financial position as 'God's will'. To my mind, they would be better advised to recognize that each of us has the power to change our situation with determination and hard work. There are very few unsatisfactory situations that we should just accept as 'God's will', when there is the possibility for us to do the work necessary to change and improve it.

The majority of Jamaicans identify as Christian and claim to follow a Christian lifestyle. There are minorities that practice other religions, but they are few. The Christian church is a powerful political force in Jamaica. Many Jamaicans consider the church, whether broadly speaking, or their specific church and its pastor, a higher authority than any other. Every Jamaican politician knows that the church's position on any social and political matter, whether it is a legislative or policy debate, or who to vote for in an election, can be critical to which way the debate or the election goes. This is a fact of life in Jamaica; it is deeply ingrained in the way we function as a society and as a country.

My critical and objective understanding and questioning of the church as an institution and its roles and its paradoxes are not in conflict with my own personal belief system. My core

Christian beliefs, my readings of the scriptures, and regular attendance at Sunday church services are still important to me on a personal level.

I like to think that what I learned throughout my years of going to church and bible study about love, tolerance, forgiveness, empathy, charity, and understanding has helped to shape me. I have worked on myself to not hold grudges; if someone wrongs me, which in politics is par for the course, I am generally quick to move on. I aim to position myself above the fray as much as possible. There is no value in living in the past, and in any situation one's best option is always to move forward positively. In all this I am a work in progress, but I try to remember to ask myself, what would love do?

I am still on my own personal spiritual journey. I am always striving to be a better person, to be more Christian in the broadest sense of the term – kinder, more forgiving, more positive, more generous. Especially through some of the more turbulent and uncertain periods in my political journey, it has been my Christian faith that has anchored me, helped me stay centred, and kept my spirits from faltering.

No Child Prodigy

I began my schooling at a one-room basic school in Hanbury. We called the school 'Miss Natalie School'. We had one teacher, Mrs Grant, who took us through the basics of ABCs and 123s. I must have got a good enough start there because my two subsequent years at Crescent Primary in Spanish Town were uneventful.

I was no child prodigy; not one of those children who are reading by age three and know their times tables at age four. I have never felt brighter than my peers. In fact, I was probably an average child in primary school through to the first few years of high school. It wasn't until my last few years of high school that I started to show anything that could realistically be considered promise.

After Crescent Primary in Spanish Town, my next stop was Mandeville All-Age, now called Mandeville Primary and Junior High School. The school was incredibly noisy because the partitions between many of the classrooms were chalkboards. For the younger children, the classrooms were overcrowded with hundreds of children and their teachers in one large space, all vying to be heard – you can imagine the horrible acoustics. It was often hard to concentrate and even harder to hear the teacher.

Most teachers had a leather strap that they used to administer discipline. I only got beaten once, when Miss

Dixon caught me playing a popular gambling-type game with rubber bands. I can remember the wheals on my hands. She scolded me, asking rhetorically, 'You ever see a red man like you sell in the market?' It was one of the first times that I was made aware that the colour of my skin somehow made me different, though it wasn't until I went to university that I became actively conscious of my skin colour and what it might or might not mean.

As a child, the fact that I was a different complexion than the rest of my family had no impact on me that I was aware of. I don't even remember noticing it. I had a lighter skin colour than my siblings, my cousins, and virtually all of my biological relatives in the community where I was raised. It is likely that others noticed my colour, because I would have stood out in that group, but in my immediate community where people knew me and my background, people would have known that my fairer skin did not make me any different from anyone else, or at least they treated me that way.

Comments like the one my teacher made about selling in the market, or a similar one made by my mother when I was ten and did poorly on a test, about becoming a mechanic, were my first clues that my looking a bit different from the others around me might mean something. It was many years later, when I got to The University of the West Indies (UWI), that I became more acutely aware of it, but even at that point I could not have articulated just what that meaning was.

Even now, as I am well into middle age, I am still learning what skin colour means in Jamaica, and what it means to and for me. The complexities of skin colour in Jamaica are many, and throwing politics in the mix complicates it even more. There is no denying that in Jamaica, even in 2019, the colour of your skin does have implications for how people perceive you and the opportunities that come (or don't come) your way.

But it is nowhere near as straightforward as the old saying, 'black stand back, white all right, brown stick around.'

Race is a social construct, and in Jamaica this has to be the first consideration in understanding the role that skin colour plays or doesn't play. What I have come to realize from my own experience is that while skin colour is an issue in Jamaica, it is much more than what shade of brown a person is, or what the texture of their hair is. Skin colour intersects with where you are from, how you talk, how you present yourself, and your job or occupation – and all that together creates a perception in people's minds about who you are, and that perception varies from one person to another.

For my mother and Miss Dixon, and for others of their socio-economic background and generation, their understanding of race and colour implied that being brown-skinned, as I was, meant that you would be out of place working in a market, or working as a mechanic. By virtue of my skin colour I was supposed to do something 'better' (in their estimation) than manual or unskilled labour.

Though the social context of race in Jamaica may have changed since I was a boy, skin colour is still very much an issue in virtually every facet of Jamaican life, whether overtly or implicitly. The phenomenon of skin bleaching in Jamaica shows that many people are willing and motivated to take extreme and unhealthy steps to lightening their skin colour. Their motivation is their perception that fairer-coloured skin will lead to more economic opportunities as well as enhance their attractiveness and sexual appeal. I personally find it sad that at this time in our development as a country, and after all the advances that we have made socially since our independence, that there are so many people in Jamaica who are still convinced of this.

But regardless of my feelings, they have reason to have these convictions. A 2012 study* on the extent to which Jamaicans'

---

* Anthony Harriott et al., *Political Culture of Democracy in Jamaica and the Americas, 2012: Towards Equality of Opportunity*. www.vanderbilt.edu/lapop/jamaica/Jamaica_Country_Report_2012_W.pdf.

skin colour has affected their access to opportunities and advancement suggested that lighter-skinned people tended to have more years of schooling than their darker-skinned counterparts. The study also showed that there is a tendency for income to decline as one's skin colour darkens, and that a person's food security is related to skin colour in the same way. This study suggests that skin colour is still a basis for the unequal distribution of economic and social resources in Jamaica, with lighter-skinned people enjoying an advantage over darker-skinned people.

I present a conundrum for understanding race in Jamaica, where there are codified understandings of what being brown-skinned means – the privileged upper St Andrew brown/not-quite-white, the St Elizabeth red/brown with their own proud roots, the Mandeville brown-parents-worked-in-bauxite – but I didn't fit into any of them. My skin colour – 'fair' or 'brown', or 'red' – is an anomaly considering my socio-economic background, and doesn't automatically bring with it the privilege that most Jamaicans assume comes with being brown. If it were that my skin colour automatically conferred an advantage on me, how is it that my darker-skinned brothers and sisters have achieved academically and professionally on par with me? In my case, at least, skin colour was not the determining factor in any success that I have had, and it may not have even been a significant factor at all.

My skin colour came from my father, a white Englishman. My father was not around and played no active role in my life. I carry his genes, but I don't know him; I only met him once, when I was already an adult. I got nothing of any status he might have had, and he contributed nothing material to my upbringing. I have no knowledge of what his genes mean for my personality, my behaviour, or my preferences, and all such things that pass down from a parent to his biological child.

The only noticeable legacy my father passed on to me was his whiteness. This has been, at times, a cross that I have had no choice but to bear. I had no say in the colour of my skin, and this is one of those situations where I have had no choice but to accept the situation because I could not change it.

Though my primary school experience was far from ideal, I did well enough to be successful at the Common Entrance exam for Manchester High, arguably the best high school in the parish. My first years of high school, however, did not suggest that my future prospects were promising.

POLITICAL
AWAKENING

I entered first form in 1980 and I looked forward to going to school every day, even though it meant a three mile walk or route taxi to and from Manchester High. I was a nonconformist from first through third form. My mother called me stubborn, even though I did my chores. In my adolescent years, we had something of a tempestuous relationship, as happens with many teenagers.

Something clicked when I entered fourth form, however. Merritt Henry, who was the guidance counsellor at Manchester High, knew my mother well, and she looked out for me. Merritt's guidance, together with what I received at home and from my extended family, was key to my turnaround between fourth and sixth form.

Another key factor in my changing course was the vice principal, Curlew Williams, otherwise known as 'Fat Head'. He was a stout, stocky man with a big afro. He was an authoritarian and assertive in his opinions. Most students were afraid of him. We clashed one time too many, and it reached a point at the end of third form when he threatened to have me expelled.

One day, he asked me to report to his office after accusing me of being disruptive. I somehow found the courage to ask him what it was that I was doing to deserve being expelled.

He glared at me and told me to stop walking around as if I owned the school, and that if I didn't improve my grades, I would be out.

That exchange with Williams gave me pause, in a way that our previous interactions had not. I don't know what was so different that time, but that particular threat sunk in. Perhaps because at home Mummy was repeatedly warning me that if I got kicked out of school she would send me to a mechanic shop to learn the trade.

I didn't think that I was being arrogant, as he was suggesting, and I felt victimized and misunderstood. As an adult looking back I wonder if he assumed that I was demanding colour-related privileges, though I had not yet at that point come to understand that my skin colour could bring me privilege. (Williams would soon come to know my family situation and that though I was 'brown' phenotypically, I wasn't brown socially or economically, but at this point we were not yet well acquainted.) But I also realized that even if I didn't think I was acting like a don, people perceived me to be acting that way, and I had to correct that, because other people's perceptions mattered, and could influence the course of my life at that point. These were people who had the power to make decisions over my life, and so I had to do what I could to alter the way they saw me. It was a profound realization and one that caused me to dramatically alter my attitude and how I went about my life at school.

From that point on, I improved academically, and in all other aspects, as I came into my own personhood. I wanted to belong to the achievers, I wanted approval from teachers and adults, and I wanted to experience everything. Thanks to people like Merritt Henry and vice principal Williams, I had my curriculum vitae in mind, even then. Shirley Bartley was my English teacher and she supported me in more than just my academics; she also was concerned with my social and cultural development. When I was to go to Mexico on an exchange programme she organized a walkathon to raise funds for the trip.

I have come to view this period of my life as a critical juncture, not just because I got myself on a better path, but because it was at that point that I recognized the power of my own determination to set my own course and shape my own future. Though I was still a boy, it was at that interval that I grasped that what happened to me going forward was largely going to be a result of what I set my mind to.

That realization has served me ever since. Even when I have come upon adversity, or plans have not unfolded as I intended or desired, I have always known that it is my own state of mind that would determine if I sank or swam, if I progressed or regressed.

This mindset has been the basis of my attitude to whatever I am doing, and has driven me always to give my all to whatever task confronts me. It's a mindset that drives attitude and ultimately performance. I wasn't born this way, I consciously chose this, though now I know no other way of being.

Is this an attitude that more Jamaicans could individually and collectively develop? In today's Jamaica there is a clear need for us to individually and collectively develop a state of mind that understands where we are and what we need to do to progress. The literature calls it a 'high performance mindset', characterized by resilience and relentlessness in moving forward regardless of setbacks or obstacles. In Jamaica's case – we are already supposed to be resilient – this would be a mindset that accepts where we are, does not get consumed with who may or may not be to blame, and allows us to move towards progress.

From that point, I became an A student, with a few B pluses for good measure. I joined the school band and became a singer and eventually the bandleader. I was president of the Debating Society. I had a lead role in 'Linval's Choice' for the Drama Festival and I became president of the Drama Club. I was the Sports Captain for Godfrey House. By sixth form, I was Head Boy of the school. Mrs Henry encouraged me to apply to be an exchange student, and I travelled for the first time in my life, to Mexico, for three months. In addition to Miss Bartley's walkathon we also put on bake sale fundraisers.

At the end of the first term of fourth form, Williams called me up in front of the entire school at devotions. In front of over 1,000 of my fellow students, he read out my results for the term, and spoke of my improvement from the year before. From that point on, I was a school favourite, especially with the girls. I was named a prefect much earlier than prefects are usually assigned. My future as a leader started to take shape.

So much came out of that pivotal turning point in my life. I not only enjoyed the attention, but it also increased everyone's expectations of me – everyone was now watching me, to see what I did and how I did it. And I responded positively to the challenge of meeting others' expectations. In fact, it was the expectations others had for me – my teachers, my mother, my other family members – that were a significant force in my working hard and doing as well as I did, in school and in my extracurricular activities.

I wonder now what it is that we are doing to our children, especially our boys, that their participation in school and school-related activities is so much less than the girls. The data consistently show that girls score better than boys in standardized tests from as early as grade one, with the margin of their better performance steadily increasing as they get older and progress through the school system. Girls stay in school longer at the secondary level than boys, and there are more girls than boys enrolled in tertiary level institutions. Is the education system becoming a 'channel of inequality which disenfranchises young men'?*

There is an argument that our boys are not achieving as much as our girls because, from they are young, we expect less from them. As the argument goes, we give them fewer chores and fewer responsibilities, and we demand less from them in their schoolwork and grades. This makes them less disciplined, less self-sufficient, and ultimately, less capable of joining and staying in the formal workforce.

I think we are doing them a disservice, rather than a favour, when from the outset we have low expectations of them, when we say, 'that's just how boys are'. When we see boys performing poorly and make excuses for them, we are not helping them. We are hurting them and the society at large. These are habits that are deeply ingrained in our culture, but there has to come a point where we all recognize and agree that these practices are dysfunctional and harmful, and that we need to change.

I was fortunate that my mother treated my brother and me the same as she did my sisters, and had just as high expectations for us boys as she did for the girls. Taking on extracurricular activities channelled my energy constructively and gave structure to my days. I was at school until the early evening doing one club or another, and then I went home and studied for a few hours before turning in for the night. I learned to multitask, and it helped me to focus and taught me discipline.

---

*   PREAL & CaPRI, *Prisms of Possibility: A Report Card on Education in Jamaica*. Kingston: CaPRI, 2012.

From my experience, I have concluded that extra-curricular activities are essential to the development of the well-rounded individual. I encourage my own children to participate in sports, the arts and clubs, including service organizations, and I would like to see more resources put into the school system to provide more opportunities for children to do extra-curricular activities. I know how important they were to my development, and it has been proven that the more activities children are engaged in the healthier, better adjusted, and more successful they are in all aspects of their development. It can be hard to justify spending money on what doesn't appear to be 'the basics', or 'the essentials', when many schools in Jamaica are in need of things like properly functioning toilets, repairs to broken windows so that the rain doesn't come in to the classroom, or enough chairs for each child.

But if we consider education, as we ought to, to be broader than what happens in the classroom – and it certainly is, as sports, the arts, and service learning are crucial components of the type of education that we need to be providing for our children in the twenty-first century – we will see that putting resources into more cricket bats, or a music teacher and some instruments for an after-school band programme, or materials for a fine arts studio are every bit as necessary and important as the other 'bread and butter' needs of a school.

During that time of my life I became more aware of myself; I also became aware of others around me. There were students much more privileged than I at Manchester High, who were driven to and from school by mummy or daddy, who wore Clarks shoes, who talked about trips abroad, who had the latest gadgets.

Was it strange that I never felt jealous? Of course, I would have liked those material things, but observing others who were better off gave me something to aspire to for myself. And, as often happens, even despite my more modest background, I have ended up doing much better than many of those more well-off children – something I often think about as I raise my own children in relative affluence.

That period of high school was instrumental in shaping my path, and that of my peers, just as today a child's performance in high school is such a key determinant of his future options. There were four of us boys in my small group of close friends. We did everything together – studying especially. Marlon Grant and Mervyn Wint were in the group, and they have both done well for themselves. Dr Carl Bruce, one of Jamaica's most eminent neurosurgeons, was also a classmate, and we later went to the University of the West Indies, Mona (UWI) together.

One of the boys did not take his work seriously and dropped out of the group. His choice to slack off, even though taken at such a young age, haunted him; when we met up just a few years later, he wept with regret at not having stayed the course with us and studying and applying himself.

This was also a time when I began to form my views on politics, and when I became aware of different ideological perspectives and the different ways of understanding how economics, politics, and societies were shaped by policies and political actions. Vice Principal Curlew Williams, who had been so important in my personal turnaround, was also my A Level economics teacher, and he was instrumental in my political awakening.

The economics class was two hours, and for the first hour Williams would give notes. In the second hour, however, was when things really got going. We would engage in robust discussion about the political and economic issues of the day.

Williams enjoyed being challenged on his positions, and I was extremely stimulated by the discussion and by the opportunity to take on my teacher in debate. Williams always pointed to the intersections of politics and economics, and ensured that we understood that they were intertwined and how – lessons that I have never forgotten and that always informed my political positions.

At first I just listened to the arguments. I would go to the library and do my own research. I began reading the newspapers with a more informed understanding of how things worked. Then as I grew surer of my opinions, I began to engage, contesting him whenever and wherever I could. At first I took Williams on just to play devil's advocate, but over time my views evolved and deepened, and I informed myself more in order to make my arguments stronger. Ironically, Williams leaned to the left, and perhaps it was in my zeal to counter his arguments that my own views developed to be more centrist and even right-of-centre.

The Jamaica Labour Party (JLP) was in government at the time, and Mr Williams was critical of their politics and policies. This was the denouement of Edward Seaga's time in office, and things were not going well for him politically, and the country's economy had stalled; there was a great deal to criticize.

These debates, I later came to realize, were key to my political education and the path that I eventually followed. It was an ironic outcome that Williams's greatest influence on me would be to hone my politics to be virtually opposite to his own.

I was one of the top students in A Level economics in Jamaica that year. Curlew Williams and I ultimately became friends. We kept in touch throughout the years. Some years after I left Manchester High, he told me I was one of his best students, and even though we held different political views by the end of our time together, I had done him proud.

He later left Manchester High to become principal of Lacovia High School in St Elizabeth. He died in 2011 after a brief illness. I attended his funeral at a small church in St Elizabeth. By then, I was a member of parliament and minister of government, an achievement I know he would have been proud of, and I was grateful to him for the role he played in redirecting my path and in a more positive direction.

My high school career, though it started off inauspiciously, ended with my being valedictorian at my graduation. It was a key period in shaping the professional and political path that I would ultimately follow, and in moulding the person that I would eventually become. Determined to follow my mother's example of hard work and making a contribution to society, I left Manchester High knowing that I had something worthwhile to give to Jamaica and its future, and I set about doing just that.

5

NIGHT SHIFT

When I finished sixth form at Manchester High School in 1987 I was accepted to The University of the West Indies (UWI), but my family couldn't afford the tuition, and the student loan wasn't sufficient. I had to sit out that first year, and I took a job at Alcan, an alumina refinery and mining operation based just outside of Mandeville, in the production department.

The experience of working at Alcan taught me that even though it was a good job – the money was good and there were many who were elated to be there as most of the jobs paid much better than anything similar in any other sector in Jamaica – it was not what I wanted for myself as a lifelong career. I was determined to get myself to university to give myself more options.

It wasn't just the loneliness of seeing my friends on a Saturday afternoon heading to the movies while I made my way to start the 4pm–midnight shift. Nor was it just about the bus not turning up after a late shift and having to walk from Kirkvine to the highway a few miles away with the other workers to catch a taxi to Mandeville. I just did not experience the contentment that the majority of my co-workers seemed to feel about being there. I had my sights set on university.

The Alcan experience taught me exposure to hard work and discipline in a business environment, which was valuable especially as I was still just a teenager. I worked in the production department, and it was hard work. The bauxite plant at the time ran 24 hours a day, seven days a week, on three shifts: 8:00 a.m.–4:00 p.m., 4: 00 p.m.–12:00 a.m., and 12:00 a.m.–8:00 a.m.

The money I earned went directly to my UWI tuition. I saved J$5,000 from that year and applied for a loan to make up the balance of the first year's tuition at UWI. I had a plan: to do what was necessary to earn a scholarship for the second and third years.

That year between high school and university was also significant because I met Neadene Shields, who has been my life partner since we started dating after graduation from high school. We were both attending a graduation fete in Mandeville; she had just completed sixth form at Hampton High School in St Elizabeth. She flat out ' boofed' me when I tried to talk to her, but the next day, I happened to spot her in the Manchester Shopping Centre, and I found the courage to approach her again. I walked beside her on her way into town; by the time we reached the taxi stand I had her number. The rest, as they say, is history. We got married in 1994.

Although our economic circumstances growing up were different, mine being more modest, we were both raised by mothers who had high aspirations for themselves and their children, and in families where education was a priority. My mother-in-law was a self-made businesswoman who raised seven children, all of whom have gone on to professional success in Jamaica and beyond.

After over 30 years together, I can proudly say that Neadene has been an exceptional partner. Being in active politics challenges a marriage and a family in ways that people who are not in politics might not appreciate or understand.

A politician is gone from home almost all the time. Particularly given the nature of Jamaican politics, constituents want to see their MP or the opposition caretaker everywhere. A politician is expected to attend every funeral, community meeting, sports competition, school event, service club fun day, and church celebration in his or her constituency. It is a full-time, seven-day-a-week job. If you are not prepared to do this as a politician, you will not likely win the seat. That is the bottom line.

When I entered active politics in the National Democratic Movement, we covered the entire island doing consultations, establishing support groups, canvassing, and campaigning. I was on the road nearly every day, from early morning until late at night.

If you live in or near your constituency, you have a distinct advantage over the politician who does not. When I rejoined the JLP and sought to be elected as a Member of Parliament, I lived and worked in Kingston, a three-hour drive from South West St. Elizabeth. I was fortunate to have my in-laws' home there, so I had a comfortable place to lay my head. But it meant that more often than not, I was away from Neadene and our children.

Then there is the stigma attached to being in politics in Jamaica. People automatically assume you are corrupt. It is easy for your family to be tarred with this brush, probably even more so when it is untrue. In 2010 when then Contractor General Greg Christie accused me, consultant Aubyn Hill, and the permanent secretary in the Ministry of Agriculture, of having committed perjury – a case which the director of public prosecutions threw out on the basis of it being frivolous – it had an effect on my family. My son was jeered by his schoolmates at Wolmer's Boys' School. There were other similar incidents, smaller and more subtle, but pervasive and hurtful nevertheless.

I am fortunate that my own disposition renders me impervious to those kinds of insinuations – rumour, false accusations, gossip. They don't really bother me, as once I know I am doing the right thing, I am not fazed. But it is hard on a family to have aspersions cast and its reputation maligned. Throughout my time in politics, Neadene has kept her head up and stood by me, publicly and privately, and supported our children to do so as well.

My children are the source of my greatest joy in life. I often think that regardless of what I accomplish in politics, and no matter what happens with my professional career, the most important thing I would have done is to have produced my three children. But truly, I am the beneficiary of Neadene's dedication and devotion to them. I played my part in bringing them into the world, and I love them, but because of my political career Neadene did most of the critical day-to-day parenting work, up to when I lost my parliamentary seat in 2011.

Neadene saw to their schooling, their activities, doctor visits, religious formation, social activities – everything that an engaged, dedicated parent does for their child. I normally came in on the special occasions and on the big decisions. It is far from ideal, and choosing to participate in representative politics should not mean that one neglects their family, but it is one of the inevitable consequences of politics in Jamaica. As a result of her efforts, our children have done well so far as students, athletes, singers and actors, and they are loving and kind young people with bright futures ahead of them.

My wife also contributed significantly to our family's income during my years of active politics. A politician's personal finances are almost always uncertain. Unless he or she comes from a wealthy family, or has entered politics later in life having already built up personal wealth, the politician's spouse's job and income are essential to maintaining the family.

I became engaged in active politics starting in my prime income-earning years, from mid-20s to my early 40s, and except for the time I was studying – when I was also not earning an income, and for the few years that I was at UWI – income stability has been dependent on my ability to juggle my political work with a few entrepreneurial ventures, with mixed results.

When you are out of office and on the hustings you are spending time campaigning and advocating, and none of that earns an income. Even when you are in office – whether as an MP, a minister, or both – the salary does not go far in supporting a family of five.

There is no job security. You can be fired without notice, or an election can unexpectedly be called, and you're out of a job. I know that all too well. Neadene has quietly worked all through my political career, ensuring that regardless of my political fortunes, there is a stable income.

Today, I can't claim that we are wealthy, but we have a roof over our heads and we meet our needs. We are fortunate, and I am grateful.

I am by no means unique in any of this. I have had a relatively short tenure in political life, and have made far fewer sacrifices than my colleagues in both parties. There are probably very few, in the single digits, Jamaican politicians who don't have similar stories about the personal sacrifices, the uncertainty of personal finances, and the costs to family life.

Some of the people who have held the Jamaica Labour Party (JLP) together for decades have far more stories to tell than I do – people like Ken Baugh, Mike Henry, Desmond McKenzie, Karl Samuda, Babsy Grange, Percival Broderick, and Bruce Golding, among others. They have sacrificed their livelihoods and careers for the party and for Jamaica, because they felt so strongly that there was a job to be done and that it was their calling to do it. Pearnel Charles has been through prison and more, in the name of politics.

There are two concerns to me with this being the norm of our political culture – the first is that it makes politics unattractive to many people who might otherwise have something to contribute. The tribal nature of our politics already renders the process one in which many people fear to participate. When the huge personal sacrifices required for a chance at electoral success are added in, then it decreases the pool of people willing to put themselves forward. Despite public perception, I think politicians should be better compensated, but at the same time, somehow held accountable, with consequences for non-performance and especially for outright corruption.

The other aspect of this which is particularly disheartening is that the JLP has been remiss in recognizing those whose sacrifices have built the party and kept the party together. We may quibble over the merit of their individual contributions, or we may not agree on all their positions or actions over the years, but the JLP would have fallen apart from the late 1980s were it not for the commitment, and the personal sacrifices, of stalwart party members who kept on.

The JLP should also do more to adequately pay tribute to those who have been and are the bedrock of the party, whether they are 'big names' or important organizers of delegates on the ground.

Where, for example, is the recognition of Donald Sangster? Besides his short tenure as prime minister (he died just six weeks after taking office), he made great contributions to the JLP and to Jamaica during his tenure as minister of finance, yet besides the Montego Bay airport carrying his name, there has been little done to honour or preserve his legacy for current and future generations.

When I became MP in South West St Elizabeth, I began efforts, through the Jamaica National Heritage Trust (JNHT) and the Culture, Health, Arts, Sports and Education Fund (CHASE), to restore Donald Sangster's birthplace and turn it into a museum. I lobbied for his first home to be named a heritage site and to incorporate this site and others like it, into the civics curriculum in schools.

Nothing materialized despite extensive discussions that lasted the four-plus years of my time in government. Roxborough, Norman Manley's birthplace and home in Manchester for the first few years of his life, was beautifully restored and made into a museum in less than a year, shortly after the PNP returned to office in 2011. All of our national heroes and founding fathers and mothers should receive the same treatment.

And where are the ongoing events to recognize ordinary Jamaicans who are hard working party faithful at the constituency level? There is much work to be done in this area.

I didn't know any of this – wife, family, children, politics, government, sacrifices, trade-offs – lay ahead of me when I was trying to keep up with that pretty young lady as she walked briskly into Mandeville that July day in 1987, trying to shake me off. All I knew was that, having graduated from high school I was about to step into a new phase of life, and I couldn't wait.

6

MICEY AT MONA

It was a bittersweet moment when I finally went off to university: I was excited to leave Mandeville and get out into the wider world, but I was sad to leave my mother and extended family back home.

I should have been installed on Chancellor Hall in September 1988, but Hurricane Gilbert put my start as a university student back by about six weeks. Once I finally got there I was assigned the hall name Micey. The seniors made up a poem explaining my name and for the two weeks of ragging, or initiation, any time a senior stopped me the ritual was for him to ask, 'why Micey?' I would then have to recite:

> I'd rather die than kill a mouse
> I love to see them about the house.
> About the mouse I'm very fussy,
> So I would save the mouse but eat the p...y

(I will let you use your imagination to complete the ditty.)

Hall life was a learning experience on many different levels. On hall I had the opportunity to interact closely with my peers from other socio-economic groups within Jamaica, as well as from other Caribbean islands. Having come from a relatively sheltered home environment in a small town, these new encounters and acquaintances were almost exotic to me.

As is the case with many of us who attend the University of the West Indies (UWI), I discovered my identity as a

Caribbean person on campus. I had hall mates and other friends from all the different islands, and as I got to know them I learned about their countries, and the similarities and differences between them and us. Having experienced the benefits of regional integration, and witnessing for myself what a regional university system has to offer, I became an advocate and proponent for Caribbean regionalism, particularly through the University, but also in other areas.

So when many years later, in 2013, as Opposition spokesperson on Foreign Affairs and Foreign Trade I called for the consideration of a temporary withdrawal from the Caribbean Community (CARICOM), I did not arrive at that position hastily. While I recognized that there were benefits with regional collaboration, particularly in areas such as education, security, natural disaster risk management, and international lobbying, I was concerned in particular with our trading relationship with Trinidad and Tobago. We were on the losing end of that relationship, and, in my view, it was one of the factors contributing to Jamaica's economic stagnation within the regional framework at the time.

CARICOM is one of those topics that we talk about endlessly, without things ever seeming to change much. I would bet that there are more undergraduate and graduate research papers, theses, and dissertations on CARICOM than on any other topic at UWI, regardless of campus – there may even be a study of how over-analysed CARICOM is. Not to mention the countless meetings over the years, at all levels of government, discussing the whys and wherefores of what we are doing and what we should change, yet very little ever seems to actually change as we talk about the same things over and over, year after year, decade after decade.

We debate and discuss and invest so much in CARICOM because it is an important organization, at many levels. But

Jamaica needs to stop talking and actually move in a direction that will either make its membership in CARICOM more beneficial to Jamaica, or seriously consider dialing back its participation. We somehow need to get CARICOM to focus on a few things and do them well – and there are areas that CARICOM's work is effective, particularly in areas of functional cooperation – rather than purporting to take on things that have never worked out and will likely never come to fruition. And Jamaica needs to be more assiduous in looking out for its own interests.

I had been looking forward to university as much as for furthering my education as for the freedom I would be afforded being away from home. I had in mind, before I got to campus, that I would be unencumbered by home rules, freed from my chores, and able to really spread my wings.

Yet, to my own surprise, for the most part I didn't venture too far from where I originated. I went to fetes on campus, and had fun, but I never drank more than a beer here and there. My first puff of a marijuana spliff was also my last. Besides not feeling any effect, and not particularly enjoying the experience, my internal moral compass that told me that this was not the right thing for me overrode any thrill I had thought the experience would bring.

I had my eye focused rigidly on doing well, perhaps subconsciously recalling my mother and Mrs Dixon's warnings about the mechanic shop or the market. I made up my mind about what I was going to do, and set out to accomplish it. I had to get good grades in order to qualify for further financial support, without which I couldn't stay in school. And I had to stay in school if I was going to make anything of myself.

I had a relatively simple strategy. I sought out the brightest people in my classes, and developed relationships with them so that we could study together and I could learn from them. In the process, I ended up making good friends during those years at UWI. Many of my campus study mates are today among my closest friends.

I felt weak in two subjects so I enrolled myself in an evening class put on by another friend, an ace math and statistics student on campus, who ran a lucrative side business teaching remedial mathematics. Every Saturday afternoon, instead of heading to the football field, I would head to Irvine Hall for a session of math and statistics. After each class we would drop a $20 in a box on our way out, our contribution to his efforts.

I got the grades I wanted and needed, and at the end of my first year on campus, I achieved my goal and got the Jamaica Flour Mills Foundation scholarship to complete the remaining two years.

UWI was also when I had to really confront what my skin colour meant for me in the Jamaican social context. When I got to campus, I met lots of new people and of course the first thing we asked each other was, 'where are you from?' It was at that point that I began to grasp how skin colour, how you speak, and how where you come from combine to shape people's perceptions of where you fit in the Jamaican class structure. The combination of my skin colour, the fact that I spoke English (and not Jamaican patois, at least not as my first language), and said I was from Mandeville seemed to have created a perception among the people who I met that I was someone I certainly was not.

I quickly realized that some, perhaps many, people perceived that I was upper middle class, and from an economically privileged background, because once I said I was from Mandeville, people assumed I had gone to Belair School. Belair was a private school in Mandeville that in those days was the reserve of children of bauxite company executives and the landed Mandeville gentry, as well as white (and 'near-white') Jamaicans from all over the island who boarded in Mandeville to attend the school. Yet, the closest I had been to Belair was seeing the perimeter wall from DeCarteret Road.

I am quite sure that if I spoke more in the Jamaican vernacular, people wouldn't have made those assumptions. If I had said I was from South St Elizabeth, rather than Manchester, the perception of my socio-economic background would have been different. If the shade of my skin had been a darker brown, they probably wouldn't have assumed straightaway that I had gone to Belair. This is how skin colour works in Jamaica – it is one of the ingredients that people put into the mix of where they situate you – it is part of the social construct.

I would of course say, 'No, I didn't go to Belair. I went to Manchester High School.' Though I was pretty sure what their assumption was, they didn't voice it outright. Should I have said, 'I know what you're thinking, but I'm not the person you think I am'? It would have been awkward for me to say out loud what I assumed they were thinking, so I said nothing. I wouldn't have even known what to say. I knew who I was, and where I was from. I had absolutely no shame or embarrassment about my background. I was not covering anything up or hiding anything. I couldn't manage or control others' perceptions of me – if indeed that is what they were thinking.

Did these perceptions, or misperceptions, help me in any way? Was the ease with which I made new friends, and fit into groups and gatherings due to my fair skin or my winning personality? I certainly didn't rely on my brown skin to help me pass my exams. My skin colour was not apparent when my A Level exams were graded, or when my application to

UWI was evaluated, or when my papers at UWI were being marked. When the UWI debating team that I captained won the intercollegiate competition in the US Virgin Islands, the colour of my skin had no effect. I didn't do less work because of any certainty that my skin colour would compensate for lack of studying or preparedness.

Throughout my entire life I worked for everything that came my way. I worked hard at UWI, because I had to get good grades to get a scholarship, and my hard work paid off as I got the scholarship I needed and subsequently graduated with an upper-second class honours degree. I had many classmates who have darker coloured skin than I do who are today wealthy and influential people, in Jamaica and around the world. They worked hard, as I did.

Nothing was handed to me on a platter. I didn't receive any favours or special treatment. Perhaps it was due to my mother's example, and her high expectations of me, her confidence that I would succeed. But I was also blessed with the gift of trusting and following my own mind – I knew that once I set out to do something, I would accomplish it.

My latter years at Manchester High and my time at Alcan, as brief as they were, also instilled in me that you must always have a notion of where you want to go. Even when things don't go according to plan – as has happened many times, especially during my time in active politics – it is your own mind that determines your way forward, regardless of the circumstances. It's an approach that I have tried to instil in my children as well as in the wider community of people that I interact with as I pursued a career in the public service.

Since I was a teenager I have always had a plan to move forward, wherever I am in life, whether it is as a newly minted candidate-caretaker trying to win a seat, or having been appointed to a ministry in an area where I did not, at first, have any previous experience or expertise, as an entrepreneur, or as co-executive director of a fledgling think tank. Whether by circumstance or by fate, I have equipped myself with an internal radar that is always pointing me forward, that always has me with a heightened awareness of the possibilities in front of me, and the energy to go after them.

In 1989, at the ceremony for the Jamaica Flour Mills Foundation scholarship awardees, I gave the vote of thanks on behalf of my fellow scholarship recipients. The guest speaker was the Member of Parliament for the area, East Kingston and Port Royal, Prime Minister Michael Manley. At the end of my presentation, Mr Manley gave me a standing ovation. It was a proud moment for my family and, of course, for me.

Manley had just come back into office the previous year, in a markedly different iteration of policy direction, leadership, and ideology than obtained in the 1970s, up to when the People's National Party (PNP) lost in the 1980 landslide election. The power that he had to convince people that in less than ten years he was such a dramatically different person was impressive.

Even though I was only a youth during the 1970s, I was aware that the political situation was volatile and that many people were apprehensive about the changes happening in Jamaica. I remember the Green Bay killings of 1978, and I remember watching a political rally on TV where shooting broke out and D.K. Duncan was on the ground holding a gun. As a boy these images were seared into my mind, cemented by the palpable atmosphere of fear that was present at home, at church, at school, and in my community.

Even if I didn't fully understand the context, I knew well that Jamaica was in turmoil, and the conversations around me – even within my PNP-leaning extended family – suggested that the country was in peril and that we needed to somehow be saved.

My studies of Jamaican politics up to that time had taught me that Manley's greatest power was his charisma and his magnetism with people, and I witnessed it firsthand that day. But as much as I beamed from Mr Manley's recognition, at that time my views on national and party politics were consolidating and shaping up to be decidedly in the JLP's favour.

7

MAXIMIZE
MANAGEMENT

The University of the West Indies (UWI) was an important building block in shaping my political views on Jamaica, on the Caribbean and, indeed, on the world. Some might say that this is paradoxical because the Mona Campus is considered by many to be the fount of generation after generation of leftist thinkers and politicians, yet I emerged as a member of the Jamaica Labour Party (JLP), generally regarded as a relatively more conservative political party.

UWI has historically been the training ground for many Caribbean politicians, many of whom would be considered to be leftist, if not at least left-of-centre. But my experience of UWI brought me to a different understanding of politics, economics, and development from that which UWI Mona is typically known for, with regard to the role of the state, the role of the market, and where the two ought to intersect.

Even though I studied hard at UWI, just as at Manchester High, I was involved in a number of extra-curricular activities. Besides my classes, group work, and hall life, I was captain of the debating team that won the regional intercollegiate debating competition in the Virgin Islands. I ran for and was elected president of the Management Studies Association – my campaign slogan was 'Maximize Management' – and elected vice president of the Guild of Undergraduates. The Guild President during my tenure was Picewell Forbes, a radio personality who became a Member of Parliament in the Bahamas and who was appointed High Commissioner to the Caribbean Community (CARICOM) in the Perry Christie Administration that came into office in 2012.

In my first year at UWI, I joined Young Jamaica, the youth arm of the JLP. My initial leanings were towards the JLP due to my A Level economics class debates with Curlew Williams, but that general direction was bolstered by what I was learning in the classroom in my management and business courses. The values of private enterprise and the business principles that were enshrined in the textbooks resonated with my own earlier established predispositions, and I considered the JLP to be more oriented than the People's National Party (PNP) towards the primacy of the private sector's role in economic development.

I was also becoming aware of the world around me, and was witness to the end of the Cold War, the collapse of the Soviet Union, the emerging consensus on the failures of state-owned enterprises, and the disastrous effects of centralized government economic planning. Even Michael Manley had re-emerged from opposition as pro-free enterprise.

At the time I saw Edward Seaga and the JLP's 1989 election loss as an indication of their political failures, but for the most part I agreed with what I understood to be the pro-market policies that were introduced in the 1980s. I saw their defeat at the polls as a political problem that the party and the leader had, not as a failure in their governance of the country during their term in office.

Even from the sidelines, as a political neophyte myself, it was clear to me then that the JLP had a communication problem, both within the party and in the party's interactions with the media and the citizenry at large. The weaknesses in building teamwork and showing unity, and conveying policy successes in terms that all Jamaicans could understand – these were among the internal shortfalls that cost them that election.

In my view, however, despite his weaknesses, Edward Seaga had set out to accomplish a great deal during his time in office by pursuing more liberal, market-oriented economic policies than had obtained in the 1970s. I certainly didn't think of Seaga as perfect – as a sixth former with intentions to attend UWI I had keenly watched the news when Seaga imposed the 'cess' on UWI students, when they were required to pay fees for the first time in 1986. The draconian response – teargassing the students and arresting and charging a dozen of them – that Seaga took to the students' protests against paying a portion of the cost of their education startled me. But at the same time, I thought of Seaga as someone who was *au fait* with macroeconomic analysis and knew what to do to repair the Jamaican economy given its dire state. I respected his resolve and determination to do what was necessary to get the numbers in order. He always seemed prepared and understood his subject matter. I admired his self-confidence.

Though I have since come to have a much more critical understanding of the policies that Seaga implemented in the 1980s, and especially that they were not quite as 'free market' as they were considered and portrayed at the time, my views then were sufficient to steer me in the JLP's direction. I would later come to realize that Mr Seaga preferred control over market forces rather than a true free market, and actively engaged in directing policies even at the micro level. These instincts were clearly carried over into his political leadership style, making him a strong political leader, sufficient to earn the title of 'one don'.

Another aspect of being a management student that influenced my choice to join the JLP was that over in the

Management Studies Department at UWI we were somewhat cut off from the rest of the Faculty of Social Sciences.

Management Studies was the newest programme in the Faculty of Social Sciences, and was looked down on by many of the other social scientists as having 'sold out' the university by trying to teach university students business and management. The lecturers in Management Studies were newer, tended to be younger, and were not generally from the UWI Mona establishment. They were more politically objective and independent, if they were political at all, than the lecturers and professors in the rest of the Faculty of Social Sciences and in the Faculty of Arts and Humanities, as they were then called. I got that sense as a student, and when I went back as a lecturer in the mid-1990s that attitude subtly prevailed.

I never internalized any of that bias or stigma. In fact, I benefited from it. It meant that there was more room for me, and others in the department, to think outside the UWI box, politically and otherwise. What resulted was that the rest of the faculty's students were surrounded and influenced by a worldview, and evidence and arguments to support it, that were different from what was being transmitted to us in Management Studies. And, indeed, many of those people from the other parts of the Faculty have gone on to senior political and government positions in the PNP.

When I joined Young Jamaica and the JLP, I was fully aware that the party had flaws and that the organization needed a great deal of improvement. The Gang of Five debacle in 1990 – when Seaga accused Karl Samuda, Pearnel Charles, Ed Bartlett, Douglas Vaz, and Errol Anderson of plotting to oust him – laid bare to me and to the public the internal fissures within the party, as well as the party's weaknesses in dealing with its own issues.

Then, as now, I saw political development as an ongoing process, and considered that I had a role to play in moving the process forward. That is the role of every active citizen in whatever area of society they feel they can contribute – engagement in moving the country forward, in however large or small an arena.

Young Jamaica at the time was the JLP's only youth arm, having superseded a number of earlier youth sub-organizations in the JLP such as Young Labourites, in 1972. We were a vocal group of UWI, CAST (College of Arts, Science and Technology, now University of Technology, or UTech), and other 20-somethings who saw ourselves as the next generation of JLP leaders, not an unreasonable expectation as many former Young Jamaica presidents had gone on to senior positions in the party, including Errol Anderson, Pearnel Charles, Horace Chang, and Ed Bartlett.

Among us when I was active were Dennis Meadows, Harry Morrell, and Charmaine Davis. As a regular course of activities, we met to discuss national politics, internal party matters, and to plan events.

My introduction to the JLP realpolitik came at one of my first events as a Young Jamaica member, at the July 1992 Annual Conference when Pearnel Charles challenged Enid Bennett for the post of deputy leader, against Seaga's wishes. It was an exciting time in the party; any internal election tends to generate energy as the contenders campaign. We were at the conference to represent our group, make up numbers, and keep an eye on the overall proceedings.

This was my first major political event, and while I held no brief for any of the candidates, I was excited about the challenge, the possibility of a leadership shake-up, and the opportunity that it could bring for the party's revitalization. I admired Seaga and his record from the 1980s, but I recognized that his strength of determination could also be, and was, a weakness. He often appeared intolerant and resisted others' ideas. This type of stance would make it difficult to reunite the party, a critical imperative for the JLP if it was to have any chance of winning back office in the next general election.

I was naïve, but I felt like I was going to witness democracy first-hand at the National Arena that day, and I looked forward to it with great anticipation. Because he was going against Seaga, Pearnel had to deal with strong pushback from the loyalist Seaga faction, including men dressed in shirts branded 'security' at the conference venue. And so when events played out as they did that afternoon – when a bottle was thrown at him from the crowd, and he was forced to retreat – I was deeply disappointed and disillusioned. I felt that the JLP had failed at the most basic task in the democratic process – a fair internal election, where the delegates would have their opportunity to have a say on who should be their leader.

Moreover, for me it was wrong for Pearnel Charles, a loyal and longstanding member of the party, to be treated that way. It was embarrassing for the party and it negatively impacted the party's credibility. Though things have improved since then, the JLP has not had an easy time coming to terms with some of the basic precepts of democratic politics, that an internal challenge to a party's leadership is a necessary and healthy course of action.

Although Young Jamaica gradually grew less active in the years after that, my involvement in the organization, together with all the other extra-curricular activities, kept me engaged in what was happening on campus and with my fellow students. It also served to broaden my social network well beyond the classroom.

I came to campus knowing virtually no one besides my classmates from Manchester High. By the time I graduated, I had a social network that extended beyond the Mona campus, covered the entire island, and extended into the Caribbean. I had forged strong relationships with some of my lecturers too, and many of these relationships endured beyond UWI. Indeed, some have served me throughout my career as an academic, as a businessman, and a politician.

When I graduated from UWI in 1991, I had an upper second class honours degree and a CV that would hopefully impress a prospective employer. I thought I was on my way.

8

WORLD OF WORK

After graduating with a BSc in Management Studies, my first job was as a forecasting supervisor at what was then Cable and Wireless. I was only there a few months when a better opportunity came along to work as a territory manager for a new consumer goods marketing and distribution company.

I moved back to Mandeville where the job was based, and that suited me well to be back near family. I had supervisory responsibility for four parishes: Westmoreland, Manchester, St Elizabeth, and Clarendon, which gave me an opportunity to travel the south coast of Jamaica and interact with small and medium-sized business people and the consumers who supported them.

Just as I got more from the schools I attended than what was presented in the classroom, I also learned a great deal from this job in addition to the business of sales and marketing. The job gave me critical insights on working conditions, small business operations, and how Jamaicans lived, insights that would serve me well when I entered politics.

I learned to communicate with different groups of people, and that there were nuances that distinguished each individual. Every person had a story, had their own unique characteristics, and in order for me to build effective relationships with my customers, I had to try and understand the particularities of their personalities and experiences.

One of my clients required that I engage in personal discussions with him about his family before I attempted to make a sale. His family was the most important thing in his life. He was in business for his family, and I knew that I should ask about his children and wife before we even talked about what his order was.

One customer was a cricket fanatic. Whenever a visit to him was on my schedule I made sure to spend some time before going to his shop brushing up on everything happening in the cricket world, as that was necessary for establishing a good rapport with him.

There was another customer on my roster who only spoke in Jamaican vernacular, laced with spicy Jamaican curse words, as his everyday language. He was as 'raw-chaw' – loud and raucous – as they come. The first couple of times we met I was taken aback until I realized this was just his way of talking. Once I figured that out, I knew I had to do my best to speak his language if I was going to communicate with him, so I tried as best as I could at matching his way of speaking. I rarely succeeded, and I probably sounded ridiculous, but I think he appreciated the effort.

Part of my job involved walking the shop floor as part of information-gathering. I would talk to my customers' customers as I tried to gauge market preferences and get feedback on our products. I would engage in conversation trying to assess their preferences and opinions.

As I would soon come to realize, and later reaffirm when I entered politics, we are all a product of our circumstances. We are each born into cultural norms which eventually form a part of us. Everyone wants to be understood for who they are and what they represent. Everyone wants their voice to be heard on matters that are important to them. Whether I was trying to sell a product, or convince people to choose me as their political representative, I had to first identify with the person, before trying to change their views – whether about development policy or a consumer goods item.

Once I adjusted my own mind to the fact that people's contexts are all different, and that a person's context affects how he or she thinks, it gave me an openness to and ability to empathize with other people. This turned out to be good preparation for the wide variety of people that I would soon interact with once I got into politics.

I was fortunate to get such a job having just left university. The job came with a car and that was a huge draw. I was able to afford my own place and live as an independent young man. At the time it didn't occur to me to expect any less – I had worked hard at UWI, in and out the classroom, and my grades and CV spoke to that.

In Jamaica today, many tertiary graduates have a difficult time finding jobs, much less jobs that allow them to establish themselves on an adult path to economic independence, and for those who choose, marriage and family. Add to that the burden of student loans, that despite the government contributing a significant portion of the economic cost of tertiary education at UWI and UTech, is still onerous for many.

Though I was fortunate, my finding such a good job then was not as unusual as it would be seen today. This was the early 1990s, and Jamaica was experiencing a short burst of economic growth that was the crest of the wave started by the JLP's policies in the late 1980s. Moreover, university graduates like me were still something of a rare breed – we were the privileged few – and jobs were more plentiful and more available.

Today we have many more university graduates, with the liberalization of tertiary education and the entry of so many new players. This is a positive development and education has been vital to Jamaicans' upward social mobility over the decades since independence. However, there are proportionately fewer jobs, and fewer jobs that pay well enough for a young person to live independently, as the economy has barely grown and the cost of living increases beyond wage increases.

Migration is, of course, an option, one that some 85 per cent of UWI graduates take up. But for many, even those who have the papers and the access to live overseas, migration is not seen with the rose-coloured glasses that many wore up until a few years ago.

More than ever we not only have to create employment, but we have to shift our mindsets and adjust our school curricula, at every level, towards enabling and facilitating the upcoming generations to create opportunities for themselves, and to see potential markets as extending far beyond Jamaica's shores, rather than equipping them to go out and look for a job that they are less and less likely to find.

I have been fortunate throughout my life, since I left university, always to be gainfully employed, whether in a job working for someone else, or in a venture that I have established and/or operated. I had made up my mind when I was in high school that I would make something of myself and that I would always earn a good living; it was never a question of if I would have a job, but what would that job be.

While I was a student, and even when I had a full-time job after graduation, I was engaged in my own personal entrepreneurial enterprises. While I was at UWI, I was something of a higgler, or informal commercial exporter – carrying goods in my suitcase between Florida and Jamaica. Neadene was studying in Miami, and I would regularly visit her. I quickly identified a market for Jamaican and 'rasta' craft items that small retailers in the South Florida area would onsell at flea markets and in ethnic stores.

At the time, as a UWI student living on a scholarship, that extra money I earned went a far way, and enabled me to enjoy a lifestyle well beyond what one might expect given my original circumstances, and the fact that my family was unable to contribute to the cost of my education or upkeep then. After graduation, while I was working in sales, I started and ran a barbershop business in May Pen where I leased a premises and rented out individual chairs to barbers. It turned a small profit, nothing huge, but a welcome addition to my regular salary.

I realized that I had a knack for sales and for business, but I also had an ambition to further my education, in part, because I love to learn, but also because I consider education to be an important means of improving oneself and advancing one's own prospects. So as glad as I was to be doing fairly well for myself in the working world, I soon packed up and went back to school.

9

MENTORS AND MASTERS

Throughout my life I have benefited from the stewardship and guidance of elders and mentors. Merritt Henry and Curlew Williams were instrumental in shaping my high school career and putting me on the path that I eventually followed. Before them, my extended family of grandparents, aunts, uncles, and neighbours from the village supported my mother as a single parent to guide me.

My university and post-university path was indelibly shaped by a few mentors, including and especially, Gordon Shirley and Evan Duggan, as well as Delroy Hunter.

Evan was my older and more experienced cousin; he had worked at Alcan, as I had, then gone on to UWI, and then pursued a career in academia.

Gordon Shirley, when I met him, was my lecturer in operations management in my final year in Management Studies. He had worked with Evan at Alcan when he had finished his undergraduate engineering degree at UWI St Augustine in Trinidad and Tobago. It was his first year lecturing at UWI, having just returned from the US where he had done his doctorate at Harvard.

Shirley and I had a good relationship, and a reciprocal one. He was not much older than me, even though he was far more advanced academically – a lecturer, with a doctorate, and I was just an undergraduate student. As much as I questioned him about the course material, and also about his own career trajectory, he asked me how he was doing in terms of his lectures and their content and his delivery.

My admiration for him led me to consider pursuing a postgraduate degree, as he had. An uncle of mine had always advised me that whatever I did I should always be in the top ten. I was beginning to realize that even though a bachelor's degree would be a big accomplishment for me, I would need more to really be competitive, or, as my uncle had put it, in the top ten.

After I graduated, Shirley asked me if I would be interested in applying for a scholarship to do my master's degree in the US under a UWI-USAID programme to strengthen the teaching faculty in the Department of Management Studies. He expressed confidence in my intellectual capacity to pursue a career in academia; of course I was flattered.

At the time I wasn't keen on pursuing a career as a lecturer. I did not see myself then as a teacher and was concerned about being legally bonded to lecture as a requirement for this scholarship. So I declined the offer initially and said that I would think it through some more. I, however, recommended someone else to the programme.

Delroy Hunter had been a good friend and study partner when I was on Chancellor Hall; he would also turn into a mentor of sorts. I had a tendency to get distracted by all my extra-curricular activities, and Delroy kept me on track, and our joint study sessions were among the keys to my success at UWI.

Delroy, through the USAID programme, did his master's in finance at the University of Florida, and later joined the teaching faculty at UWI; he went on to do his doctorate at University of Warwick in England. From there he took a position as a finance professor at the University of South

Florida. We have since remained good friends and have gone into business together.

As I thought about whether to apply for the scholarship to do the master's, I became convinced that I ought to expand my horizons and travel and learn more about the world and people from different cultures and backgrounds. Studying abroad I felt would give me that opportunity. Having worked in sales and marketing, I also found myself enjoying discussing and imparting sales and marketing advice to my customers and colleagues at work. I eventually decided that I would apply for a scholarship, as this would be a way for me to get the exposure and an advanced degree, and I figured I could only learn from venturing into the world of teaching. It was then that I contacted cousin Evan, who was doing his doctorate at Georgia State, and he recommended the business school there.

I set off for Atlanta to do my master's degree in marketing in 1993, a recipient of the Thomas Jefferson Memorial Scholarship. The irony was not lost on me that I was the recipient of a scholarship in the name of a US president who is considered one the USA's founding fathers, but who also was a slaveholder and man who fathered children with at least one of his slaves, though that aspect of his life is seldom discussed.

Atlanta was everything I had wanted and expected. It was a tremendous learning experience, and not only because of what was transmitted in the classroom. This was the first time I was living outside of Jamaica. I had spent a few months in Mexico as a high school student, and I had visited Miami while I was a UWI student, but living in a multicultural city exposed me to whole other worlds.

I met other people from many different countries, ethnic backgrounds, religious persuasions, and what were to me at the time, alternative lifestyles. Though most of Georgia is still very conservative and typical of the US South, Atlanta is a cosmopolitan, global city. This was the first time I saw Muslim women dressed head to toe in black, with only their eyes visible. I saw first-hand how beautiful and regal Ethiopian and Eritrean women were. And it was also the first time I was made to confront people living openly and comfortably as homosexuals.

I had left Jamaica a fairly typical homophobic young man. Growing up in Jamaica, as I did, in a conservative Christian family in a small town, and then living on Chancellor Hall for my university studies, meant that I imbibed and accepted the mainstream messages and thinking on sexuality. I was never violently homophobic, nor did I have particularly strong feelings about the issue, in part, because I was never forced to articulate any definitive position on the matter. But I felt, as I am sure many in Jamaica coming from a similar background did, that homosexuality was wrong and somehow unnatural.

Living in Atlanta was the first step towards dismantling my closed-mindedness. In neighbourhoods like Buckhead, I witnessed same sex couples, men dressed as women, women dressed as men, and many other variations on what I had been taught was 'standard' or 'normal' in terms of gendered behaviour.

Not only was I witness to people openly and comfortably living in these 'alternative' (to me) ways, I was also cognizant of the fact that they were left alone. They went about their business, went to work or school, went home to their families, socialized, shopped, and dined in restaurants just as I did. And no one bothered them, just as no one bothered me.

Whenever I am faced with a new issue or scenario, I usually trust my intuition to guide me to at least the beginnings of how to deal with it. My intellect and academic training also mean that I look for evidence to support one position or another, but I also factor in my own internal processing of a situation.

This new situation was quite shocking to me, even though I was careful not to betray such a reaction by openly expressing my feelings. After observing for the first few months, I came to the conclusion that more important than my own personal beliefs, grounded as they are in conservative, traditional values that were shaped by Jamaican Christian teachings and upbringing, was the right of people to live as they choose, and for there to be laws protecting these rights.

When Bruce Golding made the infamous comment in the BBC Hardtalk interview in May 2008, about not allowing gays in his Cabinet, it hurt his credibility among many of Jamaica's intellectual elite. The question that was posed to him by the interviewer Stephen Sackur, 'Do you not have a duty to consider people on their merits – for Cabinet positions, indeed, in any part of government?' put him between the proverbial rock and hard place.

Put on the spot, he was hard pressed to come up with an answer that would have satisfied everyone – the majority of Jamaicans who are conservative and homophobic, the minority of Jamaicans who are more liberal on the topic, much less the multiple and varied parties such as tourism interests, aid donors, bilateral partners, and multilateral organizations that work with and through the government, most of whom hold views that are based on what they consider a human rights perspective that does not hold hetero-normative orientation and behaviour as a norm to be upheld by state policy and legislation.

Golding's calculation in that moment, I imagine, was that while his response might – as it did, though I think he underestimated how profound the impact would be – damage him internationally, any other response would have hurt him domestically. And he was right, at least in that narrow regard, as the overwhelming majority of Jamaicans (nearly 80 per cent in 2012) are opposed to homosexuals having the right to run for public office.*

But in Jamaica, even though they are in the minority, many opinion leaders and decision-makers don't share that view. It was among these groups at home that he needed to shore up the most political capital, given his slim parliamentary majority and his precarious hold on the party. He fell out of favour with those Jamaicans, particularly those who vocally champion human rights causes, and the Jamaican intellectual elite, which came to hurt him later when many of those same opinion leaders across Jamaica later led the call for his resignation in the wake of the Manatt-Tivoli debacle in 2010–11. (A US law firm [Manatt, Phelps & Phillips LLP] had been hired by the JLP to lobby Washington to contest an extradition request for Christopher 'Dudus' Coke, an alleged drug kingpin and resident of Tivoli Gardens, which was then Golding's parliamentary seat.)

During the debates ahead of the December 2011 election, Portia Simpson Miller gave what was the first unequivocally pro-homosexual statement ever uttered by a Jamaican politician. There was surprisingly little sustained public outcry, despite Jamaica's reputation for being so homophobic. The human rights groups and other ostensibly progressive organizations welcomed her pronouncements, and while some churches expressed reservations, it was nowhere near as loud an outcry as similar pronouncements had attracted in the past. Despite her promises, there was no subsequent move to make any changes, legislatively or otherwise, in this regard.

Jamaica faces a predicament on this issue. *Time* Magazine infamously called Jamaica the most homophobic place on earth in 2006, though this is not an uncontested ascription.

---

*   Anthony Harriott et al., *Political Culture of Democracy in Jamaica and the Americas, 2012: Towards Equality of Opportunity.* www.vanderbilt.edu/lapop/jamaica/Jamaica_Country_Report_2012_W.pdf.

Some studies affirm this: a 2012 survey showed that 95 per cent of Jamaicans reject the proposition of same-sex marriage. But other credible research indicates that tolerance for non-heteronormative behaviours and relationships is growing. The younger generations, especially, are much more exposed to the wide range of lifestyles and ways in which people express their gender identity across the world, and the dominant North American media portrayal of these lifestyles tends to be very positive. My own sense is that a shift is happening, but slowly and subtly.

Jamaica is coming under pressure from tourism interests, and from multilateral and bilateral development partners, to change our laws and enact more policies that deliberately ease the hostile situation that homosexual and transgender people in Jamaica must contend with. In 2011, US President Barack Obama announced that the US would use diplomatic tools, including foreign aid, to promote gay rights around the world. When he visited Jamaica in April 2015, at his 'town hall meeting', he first recognized and applauded Angeline Jackson, executive director of Quality of Citizenship Jamaica, a group that advocates on behalf of lesbian and bisexual women and transgender Jamaicans, and described her as one of Jamaica's 'remarkable young leaders'. Jamaican musicians have been banned from some European countries for what is considered anti-gay lyrics in their songs. This is not a matter that is taken lightly.

Is homophobia an aspect of 'Jamaican culture' where as tolerance is 'foreign'? Golding himself (in an opinion piece published in a Jamaican newspaper in 2014) called it a 'battle for values', and called for Jamaica to hold firm against the 'intimidating power of the international gay rights lobby', which he considers to be 'at work here, there and everywhere'. As a sovereign country we should make decisions for ourselves based on our own social, cultural and religious priorities and mores, but I think that on this particular issue, if we don't adopt more progressive views, we will lose sight of the issues that we really should be working on.

While I sympathize with the majority view on the issue, I would like to see Jamaicans become more tolerant. We need to be more honest with ourselves and more open-minded about sexuality and people's individual rights to privacy and the right to choose for themselves their sexual partners and preferences. We need to be more honest with ourselves about what the real threats are to our children and to our supposed aims to live as Christians – is it homosexuality that threatens marriage, the nuclear family, and our children's sexual safety? Or is it the unacceptably high level of heterosexual sexual abuse of young girls? To my mind, these are problems that we should be holding marches and rallies and protests against.

I will live my life according to my own conservative views, and I will raise my children as such (knowing full well that they will develop their own views as they mature). But I don't judge others for their choices, once those choices don't affect or hurt others. I believe that as a matter of public policy the laws and attitudes that discriminate against people with non-heterosexual preferences are inappropriate in today's world, including in today's Jamaica.

I went to Atlanta to learn more about business, and for my master's thesis I studied the marketing of Jamaican goods and services in the US. This was well before we had the term 'Brand Jamaica'. I interviewed over 40 people in the US who did business with Jamaica, most of them importers of Jamaican goods and products.

There were three common threads among the interviewees, and these have been borne out time and time again in studies done since on Jamaica in general, and on doing business with

Jamaica specifically. First, there was a keen interest in all things Jamaican and a desire for more of all things Jamaican. Even though what we now call 'the brand' was associated with both positive ideas – our culture, music, and athletics – and negative (our crime and violence problems, namely), people were hungry to have more Jamaican everything: goods, services, content, information.

Second, there was widespread recognition that the goods and services that originated in Jamaica had a high 'taste profile'. That is, the things that we make and sell are better, or are perceived to be better, than similar things that others make and sell.

The third finding is where the most formidable challenge lies. What overrides these two huge positives is perhaps one of the most pervasive and difficult problems that bedevils Jamaica and its prospects for economic growth and development, in agriculture and in many other export sectors: our inconsistency in delivering quality goods and products on a timely basis.

From my studies, I gained a deep understanding of branding, markets and marketing, and adjusting product development to suit market needs. With my thesis research, I was able to bring together everything I had learned in the classroom and apply it to Jamaica. With that knowledge I was equipped to go back to Jamaica to teach, as well as to venture into my own business, if I so desired.

As I did in high school and at UWI, I got involved in extra-curricular activities and in various university organizations. One of the organizations I participated in, CaribSa, the Caribbean Student Association, arranged for Bruce Golding to visit the university to give a speech. This was the first time I met Golding beyond having seen him in passing when I was a UWI student in Young Jamaica.

Little did I know it then, but that meeting, and the speech Golding made in Atlanta during that visit, would eventually lead to my coming back to the same issues I had studied in my thesis, not as a lecturer or entrepreneur, but as Minister of Agriculture and Minister of Industry and Commerce.

With my brother Brian, about seven years old, at my
grandmother's house in Manchester.
Photo: personal collection CT.

Addressing devotions at Manchester High School as head boy, 1987.
Photo: personal collection CT.

Manchester High School graduation 1987.
Photo: personal collection CT.

Chancellor Hall Block A – home for three years while pursuing undergraduate degree at UWI Mona 1988-1991.
Photo: personal collection CT.

Winning UWI Mona debating team that won the inter-collegiate debating competition in the US Virgin Islands, 1989, with L-R: Roger Anderson (standing), Vanessa Hutchinson, myself, and Stephen Henriques.
Photo: personal collection CT.

With my mother Ruby at my UWI graduation 1991.
Photo: personal collection CT.

National Democratic Movement press conference, August 11, 1997.
L-R: Bruce Golding, myself, D.K. Duncan.
Courtesy of the Gleaner Company (Media) Ltd.

On my bicycle on the way to classes at the Manchester
Business School, University of Manchester, UK, where
I did my doctorate, 1999–2002.
Photo: personal collection CT.

With Edward Seaga at JLP Headquarters, Belmont Road,
after a Standing Committee meeting, 2004.
Photo: personal collection CT.

Campaigning for local government elections in St Catherine, August 11, 2004. This was the first election after I rejoined the JLP and it was an essential test of the party's viability with Golding having returned. L-R: myself, Bobby Montague, Bruce Golding, Beverley Myers-Howell, (candidate), Enid Bennett and James Robertson.
Courtesy of the Gleaner Company (Media) Ltd.

My first appointment to the Senate in 2005, here with Arthur Williams Jr, JLP Senator. I replaced Bruce Golding who had joined the House of Representatives as MP for West Kingston.
Photo: personal collection CT.

A motorcade in my first general election campaign for the parliamentary seat in South West St Elizabeth for the Jamaica Labour Party, August 7, 2007.

Courtesy of the Gleaner Company (Media) Ltd.

10

At the Lecturer's Podium

On my return to Jamaica, I went straight to work at UWI, as I was bonded to do, under the terms of the scholarship. I joined the Faculty of Social Sciences and the Department of Management Studies (DOMS) in 1995 and was assigned the undergraduate classes Principles of Marketing and Marketing Strategy. Principles of Marketing was a core course, with up to 200 students in each class, while Marketing Strategy was optional with smaller numbers of students.

I enjoyed teaching, and for the most part I got good feedback from the students, both directly and on my teaching evaluations. I always felt a huge sense of accomplishment when I finished a lecture. It was a great feeling to be a part of what I knew was one of their biggest life experiences and opportunities. For me, coming from a background where I had nothing to inherit, and where I had only my own mind and my own will to propel me forward, a degree was my only chance at making something of myself, and I knew that was the case for many of the students in my classes.

I pushed my students to get as much experience as they could outside of the classroom, too. Within my courses I strove to include activities like internships, group work, and presentations. And I encouraged students to get involved with as many extracurricular activities as possible, as I had done.

I was struck by the fact that most of my students were women. Over two-thirds of the students in the classes were female, and at first I wondered what this meant. This was not new – there were also many more women than men at UWI when I was a student. In 2002/2003, the ratio of female to male enrolment in undergraduate programmes was 73:27 and 68:32 at the postgraduate level. In 2007, it was 82:18 at the undergraduate level. Though there have been slight changes upwards and downwards in these numbers over the years, this is about reflective of the ratio of female to male students over the past few decades at UWI Mona. But perhaps because I was now facing the class as opposed to being in a happy minority in the midst of it, it didn't seem quite so stark to me then.

But I had, and still have questions: Why are so few men attending university? And what is the outcome and impact of this on society? What does this mean for male-female relationships? And for men's identity and security in their maleness when masculinity in the Jamaican context is so heavily defined by one's ability to provide for one's family and to be the breadwinner? And for male role models for boys?

My questions, and my observations about the paradoxes, are not original nor are they unique. The topic has been raised at nearly every UWI graduation ceremony, by one senior UWI official or another, for at least the past ten years. These are questions that Caribbean policymakers and academics have been asking for the past 20 years, and the answers are neither straightforward nor simple.

Studies have been done, conferences convened, and report after report has been written to investigate and discuss the findings, implications, and policy recommendations of the gender imbalance. Back in 1997, the Caribbean Heads of Government mandated a regional study to examine and better understand boys' underperformance. Over a decade later, the main conclusion of an extensive series of investigations, consultations, and reports was that the most critical factor in reducing risks to boys (and to girls too) was staying in school and staying connected to school vis-à-vis regular attendance, completing the curriculum, taking the requisite external exams, and participation in school activities. The challenges were to address the many different dimensions – societal, educational, economic – of why keeping children, boys and girls, in school was so difficult.*

As with many other complex societal issues, there is a great deal more going on than meets the eye – seeing so many more females than males in a university classroom is just one facet of a multi-layered situation that Jamaica and other Caribbean societies need to come to terms with.

There is much to be celebrated with the fact that women are seeking and gaining further education. This has no doubt empowered many women, economically, and otherwise. Though she didn't go to university, my own mother was the embodiment of an independent – financially and otherwise – woman who sought to improve herself throughout her life.

At the same time we are faced with what appears to be a number of paradoxes: our women are more educated and qualified than our men, and are taking up positions in middle management and outnumbering men at that level, but men still far outnumber women at the highest levels of decision-making in both the public and the private sector. There is still a glass ceiling if we look at the top tiers of business and also in the government and political party leadership.

There is no quick fix to get more males to complete secondary school, to make an effort at their secondary school exams, much less to do tertiary level studies, if men don't need higher education to get jobs that pay as well or better than the jobs that women with tertiary qualifications get. There is little incentive for boys and men to assume the financial

* Caribbean Development Bank, Caribbean Gender Differentials Framework. October 2010.

burden and time commitment of higher education when the labour market will absorb them without it, or if they will not be paid what they think their time and effort are worth.

Yet, it is problematic that men and boys don't appear to be applying themselves in school, nor care about academic success, and are not seeking further qualifications beyond high school (if they even complete high school.) It can't be acceptable that any significant proportion of a society be in obvious and accelerating decline, however they are characterized, whether by gender, race or any other criteria.

I am not an expert in education or sociology, but based on the research and my own observations I don't think it is useful to frame the issue in terms of boys versus girls. This is not a 'battle of the sexes'; both boys and girls face risks, ** though they are different risks with different causal factors and different outcomes. We should be doing everything we can to improve the prospects of all children. Where it is that boys are failing, or underperforming, or behaving deviantly, we should address those issues.

My own understanding of the problem is that it starts with how we raise boys and girls differently at home, and how boys and girls are treated in schools. We need a fundamental change in how we treat girls and boys at home and at school, and we need to understand where our traditional approaches to gender socialization – that is, how we teach boys to be boys and how we teach girls to be girls – are failing us with regard to the type of society we want to live in.

I have not fulfilled the stereotype of the fatherless boy. I have never dropped out of school or any educational pursuit, I have not engaged in criminality, and I have always been productively employed. My own defiance of the stereotype I attribute to my mother and her taking on what some would consider a traditional father role, not only in being the main

** Conference Proceedings, Regional Caribbean Conference on Keeping Boys out of Risk. Montego Bay, Jamaica, May 5–7, 2009.

breadwinner of the household, but also as the disciplinarian in the home. I also had a stable family and the support of my extended family where many adults collaborated on raising me.

My mother never privileged me or my brother for being boys. When it came to household chores, all of us boys and girls were given equal or equivalent assignments. I went to the market, washed dishes, cleaned floors, and swept out the yard as part of my own routine chores, just as my siblings did. And I managed to escape the physical and mental abuse often doled out to boys from primary school level, which is said to contribute to their later over-aggressive behaviour and their antipathy toward the classroom. Surely, my upbringing is not that untypical yet the problems seem so pervasive.

I have tried to mirror many aspects of my upbringing with my own children, though with less of the strap. But I think that at the very least, we as a society need to figure out how to address and change the widespread patterns of how many of us treat our boys and our girls.

I was a minority in the university classroom as a male student, and in joining the ranks of the teaching profession, even more so. Even though I never saw myself as an academic – rather I considered myself more multifaceted, an entrepreneur, a businessman, a policymaker perhaps – I enjoyed my time at UWI. Nothing teaches you more about a subject than preparing to teach others about it. I was always learning when I was in the classroom.

The entrepreneur in me was still active, even while I was at UWI. I had sold the barbershop venture when I left for Atlanta, but I was now able to use my new skills and training with some marketing and management consulting. I made useful contacts with industry players and business people as I sought off-campus experiences for my students, and together with the earlier contacts I had established, I was able to make forays into the business world. With my wife Neadene as a partner, I developed small business ventures which helped me to gain further experience as well as supplement my UWI salary.

Like many who experience academic life, I enjoyed the flexibility of not having to be in an office from nine to five. Granted I had 40 (or more) hours of work to do a week – it is a myth that academics and lecturers 'have it easy', and it is a misunderstanding of the work of academia that the only 'working time' is the ten or so hours a week that one spends in the classroom – but I could do it mostly on my own time, and wherever I wanted. Being on campus spoils you that way.

But pure academia was not my calling, not at that point in my life. I participated in faculty life as much as was appropriate, but I spent most of my time working on my lectures and engaging with my students and the activities I planned for them. I did not invest the time or energy into research and publishing that would have been required of me if I were to pursue a true academic career, and I was less enmeshed in the more abstract philosophical and political debates that my colleagues seemed to have been more consumed by.

I was also becoming quickly and deeply drawn to national politics, and in no time I found myself on the campaign trail.

11

NDM

In 1995, the Jamaican political climate was in flux, mainly because Bruce Golding, then Jamaica Labour Party (JLP) General Secretary and viewed by many as Edward Seaga's heir apparent, was increasingly at odds with Seaga and the senior leadership of the JLP. The entire country watched as bitter internal fighting spilled out into the public arena. The disarray suited the People's National Party (PNP), dismayed JLP supporters who didn't have a stake in the battle, and disheartened those Jamaicans who didn't align themselves to either party but who wanted Jamaica to have a healthy democracy.

The tacit expectation was that I would rekindle my association with the JLP when I returned to Jamaica after doing my master's degree in Atlanta. That would have been the logical next step since I had been a member of the JLP, had joined Young Jamaica at UWI, and had been a member of Young Jamaica's executive.

Even though many of my extended family leaned more to the PNP than to the JLP, my own orientation since sixth form was to the JLP, in large part because of my belief in the role of private enterprise in a country's growth and development. When I made the gaffe at a 2002 election campaign rally in Sam Sharpe Square in Montego Bay by saying, 'put your X beside the head!' many people took that as proof that I had originally been PNP, but I was never a member of that party. That unfortunate episode I attribute to political inexperience, nervousness, and, perhaps, too much white rum.

Not that I had or have anything against the PNP. There are excellent people in the PNP, many of whom I admire. I have friends who are PNP members and supporters. In my view what is important is that people who are called to serve, do so. It is important to a democracy to have contending views embodied in different political movements. Just because people are in different parties doesn't mean that they are at odds on everything. There are many issues on which the PNP and JLP would probably agree, if it were not for the culture of tribalism and divisiveness that governs Jamaica's political system. Apart from the tribal cultural divide that separates both political parties, the difference between the PNP and JLP today is less ideological, less policy based, and more about which party is best able to administer sound social and economic management of the country.

I had the opportunity to get a closer look at Golding the previous year, when I was in Atlanta, and CaribSa, the Caribbean Student Association at Georgia State, had invited Golding and his wife, Lorna, to come for an event. I had only had a passing acquaintance with Bruce Golding when I had been in Young Jamaica. Of course I knew who he was, though he probably didn't have a clue about my existence back then. We had invited him to address Young Jamaica's annual general meeting, at about the time that P.J. Patterson had taken over the leadership of the PNP, in 1992. Golding got into some trouble for the speech that he made that day. He called Patterson a boy doing a big man's job, and many considered it disrespectful. To my mind it highlighted a certain sensitivity and insecurity that Patterson felt, as the language Golding used was nothing unusual for a political speech in Jamaica. He must have struck a nerve. When Golding resigned in 2011, a PNP official brought up that exact same line, nearly 20 years later; clearly the PNP had never forgiven him for that.

The Bruce Golding I met in Atlanta in 1994 was a different man from the Golding who spoke at that Young Jamaica meeting. Gone was the populist politician, spouting convenient half-truths to try to please an audience. This was a man on fire, yet thoughtful and reasoned.

He gave a speech about Jamaican politics and how it was flawed, and needed to be changed. He spoke a lot of uncomfortable truths, and he did not exempt himself from his own role in them. Later on it was clear that this was the beginning of Golding's own path to what we would later call the Reform Agenda, but at the time, all that he said was new to me.

I had never before heard such a clear explanation about what ailed Jamaican politics, nor had I considered the types of changes he was suggesting were necessary to strengthen Jamaican democracy and resolve our ongoing problems of economic stagnation and crime and violence. All of us who heard the presentation were struck by it, but it resonated deeply with me and I couldn't stop thinking about it afterwards.

Shortly after my return from Atlanta, I re-engaged with members of the JLP and soon enough, through Ed Bartlett's initiative, I met Edward Seaga for the first time. There was a group of us, including Andrew Holness and Ronald Robinson. Bartlett was, on Seaga's behalf, attempting a recruitment drive for young people to join the party and rejuvenate it as a step towards resolving the JLP's internal crisis, and especially the threat to Seaga's leadership. Seaga was vulnerable having lost so many elections since 1980, and his leadership was being questioned all around, not only within the JLP. He was under pressure to step down.

There was a suggestion – in the way that such things are alluded to in situations like these where you think you know what is being said, but you are not one hundred per cent sure, and the phrasing is such that the person saying it could always deny it later – that I might run for the JLP in the Central Manchester constituency in the next elections.

As a youngster and relative newcomer, I was not involved in what was happening in the JLP at the time. It was only later on that it became clear that the meeting with myself and the others, and the recruitment drive as a whole, were a part of Seaga's effort to shore up support for himself and strengthen the party against the challenge from Bruce Golding.

Even though there was a broad consensus, both inside and outside the party, that Seaga should step down from the leadership of the JLP, there was division about who would succeed him, and it was that splintering that preserved Seaga's position. Seaga effectively exploited these fissures to maintain his position as leader. Seaga had done three consultations with JLP delegates, across the island, in an attempt to rally a vote of confidence in his own leadership. Though the outcome of his road show suggested that he still enjoyed the support of the delegates, it was nevertheless painfully evident that he was against the ropes and politically very weak.

Even though there were a few possible candidates to take over from Seaga, Golding was his biggest threat. Golding had become increasingly vocal about the problems facing Jamaican politics, and he had not left the JLP out of the equation, describing the two major political parties as private clubs. Eventually, Golding seemed to have concluded that if he didn't leave the JLP on his own accord, he would have been kicked out, and he was trying to figure out how to leave the party but pursue his newfound political convictions.

After I met Seaga, I was invited to another meeting, this time with Bruce Golding. He was having a series of meetings at the Terra Nova Hotel. The meetings were in effect consultations with different people and groups, about his political ideas and the stand-off in the JLP, and how to reconcile the issues he was facing and move forward with his reformist ideas.

When Golding and I met, he told me that he was giving thought to forming a new party and why the politics needed to change; he wanted me to come on board. I had already been reflecting on many of the issues he was concerned with, since I heard him speak in Atlanta. I was persuaded by his analysis of Jamaica and why we missed so many opportunities to move forward, why we were so plagued with criminality and deviance, and why we were so challenged by job creation and economic growth.

I consulted with people I trusted, family members, friends and some of my colleagues on campus, and decided to join Bruce Golding in whatever he was going to do. Mr Seaga was of course not pleased with my decision. He had given me some documents to review and quickly sent back for them. It was clear that I had fallen out of his favour.

This was not to be the first time that I bucked Seaga. We found ourselves on opposing sides again in 2002 when I re-joined the JLP and ran for the presidency of G2K. Nevertheless, I have always maintained a respectful relationship with him. I never took anything he did or said against me personally, as I always understood him to be looking out for his own political survival, and that of his party. In Jamaica, as perhaps anywhere, if you can't separate your emotions and personal feelings from what people say and do in the name of politics, you will find it difficult to stay sane and to keep doing the work. It is not a task for the sensitive or insecure, or for anyone whose feelings are easily hurt.

I joined the steering committee convened by Golding to consult with Jamaicans across the island and in the diaspora, to get a sense of what people were thinking as we planned a way forward. We had subgroups that concentrated on studying and discussing issues that we felt were important to the party's formation and reason for being. We spent many late nights at NDM's headquarters at Haughton Avenue, meeting people, debating, talking, fundraising, building the party from scratch. It was exhausting but exhilarating.

This was a major turning point in my political awakening and in my life. This was really my formative training ground in understanding Jamaica, its challenges, and the role of politics in addressing our challenges and moving the country forward.

The work of the steering committee involved talking and debating with hundreds of people from all walks of Jamaican life about development and change and possibility. It was a once in a lifetime experience, and has served, in many ways, as my foundation for how I have proceeded in my political actions since then.

Once Golding announced the formation of the National Democratic Movement (NDM) and shared its goals and the word began to spread, many Jamaicans were inspired and mobilized. It was one of the most hopeful times in Jamaican politics, probably the most hopeful since independence in 1962. For many Jamaicans, the NDM was offering an alternative to what was considered corrupt and ineffective politics that had seen Jamaica deteriorate rather than develop since independence.

As we soon came to realize, the dissatisfaction with the state of Jamaican politics was shared by people in the JLP and PNP also. It was more than just a difference of views among people within the JLP. Many Jamaicans, of all political persuasions, shared the sentiments that Golding expressed.

Besides the JLP members who joined the NDM, there were PNP stalwarts who also joined the movement. D.K. Duncan, Dickie Crawford, the Vassell brothers from St Elizabeth – all people who were like institutions in the PNP.

They not only joined the NDM, but also took on high profile, leadership roles.

Many people who had been a part of the New Beginning Movement, which had formed in 1992, either joined the NDM or supported it. Many of New Beginning's ideas, chiefly the need for constitutional reform and the imperative to remove tribalism from politics and reform the political system, became cornerstone positions of the NDM. There was also a Constitutional Reform Network group that emerged around that time, advocating along the same lines.

Many of the ideas that formed the foundation platform of the NDM had already existed, but the NDM took them from small verandah meetings of intellectuals and like-minded folk to the national stage, to all Jamaicans, and sought to mobilize these ideas through politics, a new and different type of politics from what Jamaica was accustomed to.

We set principles and objectives that undergirded our policy proposals, namely the dismantling of garrisons, improvement of governance, a check on executive power, a more autonomous civil service, and more autonomous state institutions. We wanted to transform the nature of Jamaican politics from an exclusive club to a more inclusive and representative way of addressing national issues and working together as a nation.

The NDM generated tremendous excitement. We were well received among most of the audiences that felt the need for change and saw the NDM as an opportunity for that change. But the popularity and traction that Golding and the NDM gathered created vehement anger in the JLP. Perhaps in the PNP, too, but if so, they were much more discreet about it. JLP members and supporters felt Golding had betrayed the party, and that his success was a threat to their own viability. This angry response fuelled and cemented the division between Golding and Seaga.

I found it remarkable then, and to this day still I admire Golding for this, that despite all the insults hurled at him from the JLP and from Seaga, he never once said anything disrespectful about Seaga, not publicly nor privately. Yes, he disagreed with his politics and his leadership of the party, but Golding never got personal. I have tried to follow that example.

Despite my role in the steering committee and being so visible and vocal, I did not win an elected position in the first vice-presidential contest in the NDM. There were four positions and 13 contestants. I came fifth behind Wayne Chen, Shaun Reynolds, Hyacinth Bennett, and Joan Gordon-Webley. I subsequently successfully ran for deputy general secretary.

The position did not really matter though – we were all so united in our common purpose that the work and the commitment were there regardless of what a person's title was or wasn't. This was just one of the beautiful aspects of the NDM. Yes, there was a hierarchy, but people weren't there for titles or positions. They were there to do the work, to try to make change. There was a purity to their motives that I have never seen or experienced since, and I will always hold dear the memories that such attitudes are possible, because I witnessed them myself. There were scores of people who contributed who never held an office in the party, who were never public about their involvement. They were passionate about the possibility for change, and wanted to do their part in trying to bring it about.

One of our first tasks was to be eligible to contest a national election. We had to have 50,000 signatures to get on the ballot.

That took us across the island and helped to canvass more support and spread the word. I discovered parts of Jamaica I never knew, and met Jamaicans from all different walks of life. The outpouring of positivity was electrifying. The desire for change and the hope that the NDM would be the vehicle for that change kept us going.

We ran a full slate of candidates in the 1997 general election and we had high hopes, if not to win, to at least win enough parliamentary seats to cement our position as a viable third party and as an opposition in the Parliament.

I spent the day of the election in Westmoreland with Russell Hammond, a former JLP MP who had joined the NDM and who was one our best hopes for winning a seat. I watched the returns at Russell's house, and the mood darkened as the evening progressed and the votes were counted.

None of us expected the outcome. Not a single seat and only five per cent of the national vote.

We were devastated.

The next day I took my car to wash it at a river just outside of Savanna-la-Mar. It wasn't just that the car was dirty, I needed to get out and distract myself a bit. I listened to the people around me discussing the outcome – no one recognized me and they were chatting freely.

From what they were saying, it seemed like we never had a chance. I couldn't understand how we could have miscalculated so badly. We thought we were connecting so well with so many people, yet the outcome, and the conversation I overheard, suggested that we were idealists who were out of touch with reality.

We had put so much into it, and gained nothing, it seemed.

A few days after the election, the party met to discuss what had happened. Though there was never a feeling that we would have won the general election, we had been confident that we would win at least a few seats. That was the goal: to establish ourselves as a viable opposition, and maybe even be the tie-breaker between the JLP and the PNP.

Bruce Golding, Brascoe Lee, Russell Hammond, Wayne Chen, Andre Foote – those were seats that we were counting on winning. We got good turnouts in those constituencies – double-digit percentages of votes – and in a few others, but the fact remained that we didn't win even a single seat.

We reflected soberly on what had happened. As we assessed the election result, we felt our message was relevant and worthwhile, but that was not enough. We thought we were going to be the first third party to break the trend of third party failures in Jamaica, but we were wrong. We considered the extent to which limited resources, and lack of an entrenched party structure had been obstacles to our doing better than we had. We accepted that the perception of winnability was a key factor in people's willingness to cast their vote for us. It seemed that there was a strong sense among voters that their vote would have been wasted and they were not willing to use their vote to just make a statement.

Another key factor was that the NDM did not have any patronage to distribute should it have won a seat. A core principle of the NDM was that patronage was a key element in Jamaica's corrupt political system, and that its elimination was essential to reform. While many Jamaicans might have agreed with this in theory, the harsh reality was that patronage was, and still is, too embedded in our system for voters to be willing to do away with it so quickly.

There was a falloff in the NDM's membership almost immediately. People were disappointed and lost hope, but it was more than that – people had to go back to their lives. Most of the people who had joined the NDM and had worked so hard were ordinary Jamaicans, not career politicians. That was the beauty of the movement. Jamaicans who had never been involved in politics before came out and got involved.

But that strength was also our weakness. These same 'ordinary people' had jobs and businesses and families that had been put on hold for over a year as we built the party and campaigned for the election. People had to rebuild their lives. Unlike lifelong politicians in the JLP and the PNP, they couldn't see a viable political future ahead, and for them there was no alternative.

I still had my job at UWI, which afforded me the flexibility to continue working with the party. I was in a relatively unique situation, compared to the others who had businesses or employers who expected them to hold regular office hours.

Seaga reached out to me after the election and I met with him at his office in New Kingston. He invited me to re-engage with the JLP. I replied that I would be prepared to go back but a space had to also be made for Bruce Golding and the NDM's reform agenda. That put an end to the conversation, at least for the time being.

When Reverend Herro Blair, who was NDM chairman and an important inspirational force in the movement, left the post and the party shortly after the election, I took over as chairman. It was a lonely job. Sometimes I felt like I was one of a handful of persons running the NDM. Even those who had not completely dropped out were busy getting their lives back on track. There was no election in the offing, and there didn't seem much point to devoting the time and energy necessary to continue to build the Movement.

I persisted because I believed in the NDM and what it stood for, and I felt that our goals and objectives were still relevant and necessary for Jamaica. I too, though, had other business to take care of. I had just turned 30, and there were still a lot of stones left unturned in my own life.

12

BY-ELECTION

In 1999 I was awarded the British Commonwealth Scholarship and was accepted to the Manchester Business School, University of Manchester, in England, to do my doctorate.

I was torn about relinquishing my role in the NDM and thought hard about what to do. I still felt that the NDM's agenda was relevant to addressing the challenges Jamaica faced, and did not want to appear to be abandoning the cause that so many people fought for and still believed in. It was a choice between me and my family's personal development, and the continued commitment to the many colleagues and supporters who felt strongly about the need for a political reform agenda.

I was also concerned about leaving my responsibility and commitment to Bruce Golding, the founder and leader of the movement. I could feel at that time that he himself was struggling with what his next move would be in his political journey.

My estimation of his situation was that while he remained committed to his cause, he was questioning the practicality of his mission. Though this was never expressed to me, I discerned that he was having doubts about the prospects of Jamaica's 34th attempt at making a third party accepted by the Jamaican people.

The NDM was in a slump after the 1997 elections, and there would still be three more years before another election was expected. I decided to move on to higher learning because I felt at the time it would place me in a position to acquire knowledge and give me greater exposure to the world. My political instincts were also at work as I calculated that I could complete the doctorate and get back in time for the next election.

I was further encouraged because even the most loyal members of the NDM persuaded me to go. They assured me that the Movement – and the country – would benefit more from me advancing myself, than if I were to stay.

I resigned from the chairmanship and moved with my wife and son to England and started at the Manchester Business School.

Stafford Haughton, a former JLP Member of Parliament for the constituency of North West Manchester took over as chairman. I had recommended him to Golding when I discussed my decision to give up the chairmanship. Though I was not physically in Jamaica, I kept in close contact with my colleagues and I was still able to participate in some of the discussions within the party.

Then came the North East St Ann by-election in February 2001. This was, it turned out, the litmus test to see if there was a viable future for the NDM in Jamaican politics. I broke my studies and came from England to join the effort. It was that crucial. It was to be the final test for me, and for many of the others who had remained in the NDM post-1997. A final attempt whether or not the NDM had any realistic future as a meaningful political force in Jamaica.

It was the ideal seat for us to contest. Its outcome would have no meaningful effect on the parliamentary seat split or the existing balance of power between the PNP government and the opposition JLP. The idea of people 'wasting' a vote ought to not have been a significant factor, or so we reasoned and convinced ourselves.

We had a great candidate. Barbara Clarke was originally from the area, a self-made businesswoman who was politically savvy and charismatic. She had come from a stalwart PNP family before joining the NDM.

Two other women contested the seat – Shahine Robinson from the JLP, Carol Jackson from the PNP, and a Rastafarian, Ras Astor Black. I am sure it was unprecedented then in Jamaican electoral history that three women and a Rastafarian were the contenders for a parliamentary seat.

We put our all into it. Every active NDM member, and a few who came out of the woodwork, was on the ground, campaigning, canvassing, working. Our fundraising had been successful and we could not claim that lack of money had kept us from doing something that could have helped us win. We covered every inch of that constituency; no stone was left unturned. Every person who had an interest in seeing the NDM succeed contributed to the effort – we all wanted to see if the party indeed had a future.

And again – five per cent of the vote.

At that point, most of us accepted that if we wanted to see political change in Jamaica, in our lifetime, the NDM was not going to be the vehicle for that change. We would have to find another way to do it. I saw this very clearly, that if I wanted to participate in Jamaican politics in a way that would make a positive difference, the NDM was not the party for me to work with.

Before I went back to the UK, I met with Golding and told him we are at a crossroads. The NDM has great ideas and good people who are committed and want to contribute to nation building; we have given it our all. The Jamaican political culture is too steeped in the two-party tradition. We have to look at what possibilities exist for these good people to engage in the existing political process and see what difference they can make from within the PNP and JLP, or civil society.

Even though Golding didn't publicly accept my assertion at the time, I believe the concerns I expressed were not lost on him. He resigned from the NDM a couple of weeks later, in March 2001. Educator Hyacinth Bennett took over as the NDM's leader. Barbara Clarke subsequently re-engaged with the PNP, representing them in North Central St Andrew in the 2002 election, though she lost to long-time MP Karl Samuda. Bruce Golding began a stint as a radio talk show host. Most everyone else returned to private life or to the political parties whence they came.

But not all the critical players of the NDM at that time felt the vehicle of the NDM should have been abandoned. There were some in the party, and outside the party, who felt it was too short a time to judge our having succeeded or failed, and that we should and could have gone further. But not all who desired continuation were willing to do the work necessary to keep the movement alive and viable.

The fact was that this was a tremendous amount of thankless, time-consuming work, with little beyond an election by which to measure progress. No political party can exist without financial and popular support, and we had lost a great deal of both after two overwhelming electoral defeats. Funding would have been virtually impossible from that point on. The NDM has continued to exist but it has never regained its position as the force it had been when it started.

I have no regrets about the time I spent in the NDM, or the work I did. I learnt a lot about Jamaicans and Jamaica during this period. It was a unique training ground in Jamaican politics, and I met a cross section of Jamaica's most excellent citizens, many of whom I call my friends today. Virtually every person I know who was involved in the NDM has fond memories of those years, and agrees with me that it was time well spent. I will never despair for Jamaica because I met so many good people through the NDM.

I enjoyed the road, travelling with Bruce Golding and others to spread the word for political change, and visiting every square mile of the island of Jamaica – I don't think there is a single district that I have not stepped foot in. Bruce Golding was a good teacher, and I learned a great deal from him, including perseverance and excellent oratory. He convinced many Jamaicans from all socio-economic groups that he had a vision for Jamaica. I hope one day to be as articulate a speaker, as able as he is to synthesize complicated issues into understandable messages that convey the elements of the problem or issue, but also impart hope that change is possible.

Aside from my own personal experience, I am also proud of the NDM's contribution to positive changes in Jamaica's politics. We may not have won any seats in Parliament, but the NDM transformed Jamaican politics and governance in ways that we as a country are yet to fully understand, and are still benefiting from.

Of course, there are things that, knowing what we know now, we could have done differently, but there is still a great deal that we accomplished. In the context of Jamaican political history, we fit into the general pattern of third parties, not having been successful at the polls, though we were one of the strongest. But I think we were the most successful, as many of our positions have been made into state policy.

We never held office, but we introduced a new platform of ideas to the Jamaican political debate, bringing to the fore the importance of participation and transparency, and the detrimental effects of political tribalism and political violence. The overarching objective was to make Jamaican politics more democratic and more participatory, and ultimately, move Jamaica forward to better fulfil its development potential, and to bring about better living conditions for all Jamaicans.

Before the NDM, these were not widely acknowledged issues in Jamaican politics, and they were not well understood by the majority of Jamaicans. We opened the door to the recognition and understanding of these fundamental dysfunctions in our political system. It was the NDM that introduced the ideas of corruption, transparency, and accountability to the Jamaican political conversation. It may seem impossible today that we haven't always been talking about these issues, but prior to 1996, those were unheard of in the political dialogue. The NDM raised awareness about these issues among the electorate, inserted them into the political agenda of the major political parties, and in so doing, began the process of changing them.

In its rejection of political violence, one of its main platforms, the NDM can be credited with a dramatic fall in election violence. The year 1997 marked the first time where election violence was an exception to the Jamaican norm since 1976. This was noticed not just in Jamaica, but around the world.

We can attribute the formation of the nonpartisan monitoring group called the Citizens' Action for Free and Fair Elections (CAFFE), comprised of religious and civic groups who came together and trained more than 2,000 poll watchers, to the NDM and the heightened awareness of the need for violence-free elections. In 1997, we had international election observers for the first time. We may take this for granted in Jamaica 20 years later, but none of this existed prior to the NDM.

The NDM revitalized engagement in the political process at a time when many Jamaicans were apathetic about politics. The caucus to collect 50,000 signatures to qualify to be placed on the ballot as a third national political party was not an insignificant exercise. In seeking out those signatures, we educated people and brought people into the process.

Nearly 200,000 more people registered to vote between 1993 and 1997, and 100,000 more people voted in the 1997 election than in the 1993 election. The number of people registering and voting was greater than the increase in the number of people of voting age from 1993 to 1997. This was a direct result of the NDM's mobilization of uncommitted and disinterested Jamaicans.

We also created a new crop of civil society leaders who got their start in the NDM. Aside from mobilizing signatures and uncommitted voters, we brought people who had never been involved in politics into active engagement in the party. Many of these people had foresworn politics for its violence, its tribalism and its corruption, but the NDM presented them with an opportunity to get involved in an untainted political organization.

Once the NDM ceased to exist as a viable political party, many of these people started their own civil society organizations or took leadership roles in other groups that advocate for better governance. As a primary example, Herro Blair, a popular charismatic Christian preacher and leader entered party politics, unprecedented for a churchman of his standing, as the NDM chairman. He continued in a prominent national position for over a decade after leaving the NDM as he was appointed political ombudsman by the PNP government in 2002. Yvonne McCalla-Sobers formed Families against State Terrorism (FAST), Carolyn Gomes founded Jamaicans for Justice, Dickie Crawford has been very vocal in many different capacities and has also started an organization, Jamaicans United for Sustainable Development.

These are just a few of the people who were involved in the NDM in some way, and later went on to play important roles as actors and activists in civil society and non-governmental organizations. Jamaica is better off for all of these people's involvement in the democratic process, and I think we can fairly state that the NDM played a critical role in inspiring them to participate in public life.

The NDM's position advocating the separation of powers between the legislature and the executive (in the Jamaican configuration that would be the Parliament and the Cabinet) was a radical proposition for Jamaica. The concern was that the prime minister had far too much power, as did ministers of government, that the people's elected representatives did not play a significant enough role in governing the country, and that this situation facilitated corruption and mismanagement of the country's resources.

The objective was to create more accountability and transparency in government by re-balancing the power between elected representatives and those making decisions on the allocation of state resources and the implementation of state policy. The separation of powers proposal was a means to that end.

We have made progress in Jamaica towards better governance, greater transparency, and improved accountability since 1995. Again, the NDM was key to the beginning of that transformation, in shining the light on these issues and bringing them to the fore.

More concretely, it was the NDM's position that undergirded one of then-newly elected Prime Minister Bruce Golding's very first actions, which was to appoint opposition members to chair Sessional Select Committees of Parliament.

This was a step towards strengthening these previously somewhat ineffective committees' ability to provide oversight, and to improve transparency, because chairmen were members of the governing party. The PNP, to its credit, did not reverse this policy decision for opposition members to chair oversight committees during their term in office, 2012–2016. That alone comprised a valuable step forward in improving the checks and balances between the Opposition and the ruling party, and strengthening the role of the Parliament in general.

There is still a great deal of work to be done to strengthen the oversight committees, and the Parliament's ability to influence decision-making, but an important start has been made, and the idea for that germinated in the NDM.

Another concrete accomplishment that was in the original NDM proposals was the establishment of an Office of the Opposition Leader, with a staff, funded by the government. When Golding became prime minister in 2007, this was one of his first actions, and Portia Simpson Miller was the first opposition leader to have a physical office space with staff that was not paid for by the party or its supporters.

It is unlikely that a third party in Jamaica will ever be successful in the foreseeable future, but the NDM was not in any way a waste of time or energy. Jamaica is a better place for the NDM's existence and work, and I am a better person and politician for my experience in the NDM.

Though the JLP's Shahine Robinson won that 2001 by-election in North East St Ann, it was not the comeback that Seaga had banked on. But the election did portend massive changes in the JLP as the NDM's poor showing and its virtual collapse thereafter turned out to be a critical juncture for Bruce Golding's – and my own – return to the JLP.

13

ENGLAND

When I left Jamaica in 1999 to pursue further studies, I still had no plans or ambitions to make academia my lifelong career, but my hunger for knowledge remained.

Once again, I followed in my friend Delroy Hunter's footsteps. I had done my master's in marketing while he did his in finance, and had also gone back to UWI to teach in management studies, as he had done. Now I went to England to do a doctorate, just as he had. Delroy was much more of an academic than I was – he loved researching, writing, and theorizing. Though he knew that I saw myself as more of a practitioner, he encouraged me to do a doctorate in business administration (DBA) as an investment in myself, whether I went into academia or not.

At Manchester Business School, my supervisor was Jeff Ramsbottom, an Englishman married to a Trinidadian. He had a keen interest in the Caribbean and took me under his wing once I landed on campus. We got along extremely well, and he became my mentor and later my colleague during my time at Manchester.

Besides supervising my thesis, we collaborated on other endeavours. He invited me to accompany him on teaching assignments in the UK, as far as Wales, as he taught in the Manchester Extension Programme. Soon enough, I was also teaching in the programme, including back in Jamaica when I returned home, earning some much needed pound sterling in the process. I also taught undergraduate classes at Manchester Metropolitan, a college near the University.

The doctoral programme was all-consuming, even more so given my determination to finish in less than three and a half years, which I did: three years, two months and 28 days. Despite having received a British Commonwealth Scholarship, I could not afford to fully fund myself and my family there. I had to take on teaching assignments to supplement my income, and Jeff was kind enough to allow me that opportunity. Financial considerations aside, I still closely followed the political scene in Jamaica and kept myself in the loop as much as I could.

The time in Manchester was well spent. The days were long and sleep was a rare and precious commodity, but I thrived. Aside from acquiring the doctorate, I got to experience life in Europe. It was a completely different lifestyle from what I knew from Jamaica and even the US – initially a bicycle was my main form of transportation, but eventually I bought an old Ford Escort that could hold the family.

I once again found myself in the midst of people from all over the world, with over 30 different nationalities at the Business School. The culture was diverse and the experience rich, particularly when having a pint of beer at the pub downstairs in the centre of the Business School or on the streets of Manchester where Friday and Saturday nights saw the streets packed with revellers enjoying beer and music.

Manchester is a student town, with five universities and approximately 50,000 students within a close range, so there was always something fun to do. The city is the proud home of popular football teams Manchester United and Manchester City. It is also the city of Old Trafford cricket grounds. I used the opportunity to visit all three sports grounds to watch games, and I became a Manchester City fan, perhaps because they were underdogs at the time, but I also enjoyed the profile of their supporters, primarily blue collar, fish-and-chips-eating Brits who never missed an opportunity to be loud at the games. It was electric to be a part of over 30,000 fans chanting and shouting during a game. I felt as if I belonged, even though I was a newcomer and a foreigner.

My Old Trafford experience to watch England play the West Indies may have had more significance than I originally thought. My oldest son Charles was an avid sports fan since he was a little boy, but I credit that experience with him at Old Trafford for motivating him to excel in cricket. He played on Jamaica's under-15 cricket team which won the Caribbean Cricket Tournament in 2009.

I am also grateful for my English experience for Neadene. While we were there, she supported me in my studies, kept our home happy and comfortable, gave birth to our second child, our daughter Kimberly, and completed her master's degree in logistics management at nearby University of Salford.

Another important event happened when I was in England: I made my first contact with my father. My father was a myth to me. Then again, the word myth is not really appropriate. A myth suggests that a story has been created and reinforced over time so that it becomes almost close to the truth. My mother had not told me stories of my father, and no one else in my life had ever spoken about him. I knew nothing about him.

Nor can I say that my father was a mystery to me, because I did not think about him very much, at least not consciously. When I was a child, Mummy never mentioned him, and I – for reasons that are not apparent to me now and I don't know if I will ever care to explore – never asked much about him.

I didn't wonder who he was, what my life might have been like with him in it – though it would likely have been very different, as I later came to learn – why he left, why he never claimed me, or even if he ever thought about me. As a child, I was too young and too happy to know that I was supposed to have a father, and since no one pointed out that I was missing one, I didn't think anything was abnormal or out of place.

There were many other children around me who didn't have fathers, and my life was so full of other people – grandparents, aunts, uncles, cousins, siblings, and neighbours – who were physically present, and who loved and supported me fully and unconditionally, that I never felt his absence.

But when I was 12 or 13 I began to wonder about him. I asked Mummy and she told me that he was from England and had been in Jamaica working as a civil engineer with one of the bauxite companies. From that brief conversation, I got the sense that Mummy was uncomfortable. She would have been the only person to ask about him, but I did not ever want to make my mother uncomfortable, so I never asked again.

Around the time I was finishing high school my curiosity about my father resurfaced, and I tried to locate him. I found an organization in the UK that connected families, and I wrote asking them to help me. The correspondence went back and forth over many years (this was in the days before email and the internet), and they eventually sent me a state-issued document that contained his full name and a few other data points. At that point, they informed that they could do no more to assist me because they couldn't violate his privacy. By that time I was in Atlanta, and I left it at that.

Now that I was living in England, it seemed obvious that I should pick up where I had left off. About midway through my time there, I found a Tufton in the telephone directory and called. It turned out that this was my father's brother. To my surprise, he gave me my father's number, no questions asked.

I then phoned my father and introduced myself. He expressed doubt that I was his son. I tried to allay what I thought might be his fears and told him I didn't want anything from him. He insisted that what I was saying couldn't be true. Once he had said that, there was nowhere for the conversation to go. I hung up and left it alone after that. I told myself that at least I had heard his voice, but I knew that there was nothing meaningful about that and that our brief exchange of words didn't even amount to a conversation. I buried my disappointment and continued forward with what I had really gone to England for: to pursue my doctorate.

I chose to do my dissertation on foreign investment in newly liberalizing economies. I did not use Jamaica as a case study because I wanted to be exposed to other countries' experiences, and by then I was familiar enough with Jamaica and the English-speaking Caribbean. I wanted to learn what other countries had done so I could see what lessons could be learned for ourselves.

I chose to study the experiences of the Czech Republic and Cuba, two countries coming from similar Communist systems, but each choosing different paths to liberalizing their economies. It was a comparative study, and my goal was to understand how the different paths to liberalization worked.

For each country, I looked at industries that had previously been state-owned, were now liberalized, and which currently had foreign investors' participation. I examined the formulation and implementation of investment laws, and studied the production processes and how they involved other countries and companies, and how the laws and policies regulated the participation of other entities.

In the Czech Republic I studied Skoda, the car manufacturing company that had been bought by Volkswagen, a German company. Though the company was now foreign-owned, the Czech laws mandated foreign investors to use local suppliers, and to work with local manufacturers to upgrade their production processes and standards to international levels. In the Czech Republic, Czech businesses worked with foreign entities to improve and raise their own standards so that they could produce at the highest standards and be internationally competitive.

I stayed in Prague while doing my field work and took a bus each day to the outskirts where the Skoda plant was located. Even though I didn't speak the language, all the managers spoke English and so I was able to interview them without language being a barrier. I interviewed executives at Czech Invest, similar to JAMPRO in Jamaica, as well as members of the local chambers of commerce. I also studied the tourism industry in the Czech Republic.

For Cuba, I examined a cigarette manufacturing joint venture between a Brazilian cigarette company and the Cuban government, BrasCuba. My other research subject was Sol Melia, a large Spanish hotel chain that has resorts in Cuba. I didn't know it at the time, but this research would later equip me well for national office, and give me important insights into policy approaches for governments when dealing with foreign investors.

For all my cases, foreign direct investment (FDI) was beneficial to the host countries. The investments created jobs, enhanced skill sets among locals, internationalized local goods and services, introduced international standards into local manufacturing and service delivery, and improved internal and external supply linkages.

But those benefits did not come by accident, nor were they all the intention of the foreign investor – the Czech and Cuban governments played important roles in negotiating the terms under which the foreigners would be allowed entry, and the conditions in which they would be allowed to operate. At the same time, the foreign investors I studied were much more willing to negotiate and make concessions to governments and their own priorities when the investors' strategic needs were accounted for by the respective governments.

The lesson for Jamaica, and other countries who seek FDI as a means of promoting economic growth and development, is that there is an important role for governments. It is their task to research and understand potential investors' specific strategic needs, and seek to meet them, and having done so, to negotiate terms that will ensure that the investment leads to multi-layered benefits in the host country. A strong and capable investment promotion agency can be beneficial to such a task.

Today, Jamaica tends to be critical of foreign investors and to view them as taking away opportunities from local entrepreneurs, or somehow gaining some unfair advantage. This is a position that is difficult to defend. We live in a global village where interdependence is standard for countries to prosper. Second, Jamaica is either not attractive enough for local investors or local investors lack the capacity to create and exploit all potential opportunities and, as such, our destination has to be discounted for foreign investors. Third, we need investment, whether local or foreign, and the issue should be how to stimulate that investment, not to discriminate on the basis of the geographic origin of its source.

I was anxious to return to Jamaica, but I knew that if I went back before I completed writing up, I would get distracted. I decided to stay in the UK and dedicate myself to finishing the degree, dissertation and all. Yes, England was full of new opportunities and experiences for my family and me, but Jamaica was home.

14

BRAIN DRAIN

In England, though I was not an economic migrant as most Jamaicans are – both of the times I lived abroad I went to further my studies – I was able to experience the life of an emigrant when I went to the US and to the UK to study. I also connected with Jamaican migrants in the US and the UK when I lived there, so I came to have a first-hand understanding and experience of life as a Jamaican migrant, and as a member of the Jamaican diaspora.

The role of the diaspora has always been at the forefront of my mind as I have thought about and grappled with Jamaica's issues and possible solutions. While the Jamaican diaspora is not a homogenous group, and should not be treated as such, I think there is still a lot of work to be done to better connect the Jamaican diaspora, broadly speaking, with Jamaica and its development.

An odd thing happened while I was a senator in May 2013; then-president of the Senate, the government-appointed Senator Reverend Stanley Redwood, resigned his position to migrate to Canada with his family. It was an awkward situation. Redwood had run for a seat in Parliament twice (unsuccessfully) and had been selected in 2012 by Prime Minister Portia Simpson Miller for one of the highest appointed offices in the country. Yet, he was leaving the position to make a new life abroad.

Even more peculiar was his parting admonition to us, his senate colleagues, to redouble our efforts to make Jamaica a better place so that other Jamaicans shouldn't 'feel forced to make the choice' that he did, to migrate, and that 'Jamaica should be further along on the pathway to be able to sustain more of the hopes and the dreams of more of its citizens.' It must have been embarrassing to the PNP that someone appointed to lead their charge in the Senate saw it fit to try for a better life abroad, right in the middle of its own term in office.

Migration is a fact of life in Jamaica, just as it is for many other countries, within and beyond the Caribbean. Even if and when we are able to get Jamaica on a path to fulfil its economic and social development so that people like Redwood won't feel that they have to leave Jamaica to realize their goals for themselves and their families, people will still be moving back and forth between Jamaica and other countries, especially the US, Canada, and the UK. Our history of migration and the interconnectedness of our families make migration an inevitable fact of our lives as individuals and families, and our life as a nation.

Regardless of conditions at home, there are benefits to be had from having an economically successful diaspora population overseas. Beyond remittances – which are essential to Jamaica's economy, particularly given our decades of economic stagnation – overseas Jamaicans can lend their skills and expertise that they gained overseas to businesses and other activities within Jamaica. There are many Jamaicans at the highest levels of the largest and most influential organizations in a vast array of fields in North America and Europe – academia, accounting, law, finance, medicine, engineering, technology, and multinational organizations. And there are also Jamaicans who have gained valuable experience working in service industries and in manufacturing, among other sectors, and their know-how and understanding of their fields can be invaluable if properly shared and imparted.

Even if we do achieve our goal, one day, of being a prosperous nation, we will always be small and always in need of ideas and resources from the outside. Having a diaspora that is connected in meaningful ways will facilitate the transfer of knowledge, resources, and skills that could be invaluable to Jamaica's development prospects.

Like many Jamaicans, I have family members who have migrated. My brother Brian was a police officer who did his undergraduate degree at UWI and joined the Jamaica Constabulary Force at a senior rank in their graduate entry programme. He excelled in the force and did a master's degree in England.

Brian's wife was also highly trained in her field of software development, and they decided as a young couple, just starting out, that their prospects to build up their economic base and provide a quality life for their children were better outside of Jamaica. It was not an easy decision for them, as I am sure it was not an easy decision for Redwood, or anyone who chooses to migrate. To uproot yourself from all you have ever known to settle somewhere new and different is one of the most drastic changes anyone could ever make in their lifetime.

Probably from the very start of the phenomenon of Jamaicans migrating overseas in search of greater opportunities, there have been attempts by successive governments to figure out how to keep them connected to Jamaica. Most of those efforts have been focused on how Jamaica can reap the benefits of our emigrants' hard work overseas, though there have been initiatives that have had the pretext of seeking to give diaspora Jamaicans a voice back here at home.

I know that it leaves a bad taste in the mouths of Jamaicans overseas that they have left home to seek to do better for themselves and their families, often enduring great hardship along the way, even sometimes discrimination, yet the place that they left behind is still trying to extract from them.

At the same time, many – I would venture most – Jamaicans who migrate want to continue to be involved in Jamaica, at some level, in varying degrees. Many overseas Jamaicans remain deeply interested in and committed to Jamaica's advancement. But how much is really achieved by the various diaspora conferences that have been held over the years? Is this the most effective way of building and maintaining reciprocally beneficial ties to Jamaicans overseas and their descendants?

My sense of these diaspora conferences is that they are a lot like CARICOM – an organization that has arisen out of a genuine need for bringing parties and interests together, but that hasn't quite effectively captured how to fulfil its mandate, and just ends up being a talk shop making unrealistic plans with no measurable outcomes.

How we make connections and build relationships that are not one-sided and exploitative to the diaspora and that are also real and meaningful and bring benefits to both Jamaica and to the diaspora in all its many manifestations is something we have yet to figure out, but I think that there has never been a better time than now to seek to do this.

The revolution in communications technology has made bridging the physical gap between Jamaicans overseas and those in Jamaica more feasible than ever. Social media especially has created a networked world in which Jamaicans anywhere can be in Jamaica virtually as they listen to the television or radio news at the very same time as those of us who live in Jamaica do. Money can be transmitted instantaneously across the world, people in two different continents can work on one document once they are connected to the Internet – the possibilities for collaboration and involvement are vast.

Think of the way that both Jamaicans at home and in the diaspora were mobilized via social media when Tessanne Chin was competing on the reality show 'The Voice' in late 2013, or how Jamaicans all over the world interact with each other on Facebook. Many businesses have figured out how to bridge the divide – Jamaica National, for example, has been extremely successful in using Internet technology and an active outreach effort to physically connect with overseas Jamaicans in their communities, to build many of their product lines.

But we are still wanting for a more accurate quantitative and qualitative understanding of the diaspora – who they are, how many they are, where they are, and what would be the best way of engaging them for the benefit of all. And how do we better incorporate the diaspora in our development planning? Do we rethink the role of the Ministry of Foreign Affairs and Foreign Trade to more fully include responsibility for Jamaicans overseas, as Ireland has done in its attempts to harness the collective influence and power of its more recent migrants as well as the millions of descendants of those who left the island over a hundred years ago?

We need to be more specific or narrowly focused on what we mobilize the diaspora community to do. Apart from making it easier to send remittances, we should look at Jamaica's most important needs and determine how we can summon the suitable diaspora influence to address those needs, but in a mutually beneficial way. We also have to be clear that the same concerns that deter foreign investors also deter diaspora investors – crime, corruption, and capacity.

Focus on economic development and package opportunities targeting our diaspora influences, give them the red carpet treatment, and leverage their reach and access to help to build Jamaica in a way that is meaningful for them and rewarding for the country. We need to attract and encourage more Jamaicans like Michael Lee-Chin and the late Raymond Chang to be part of Jamaica's development and, if necessary, facilitate them to identify with Jamaica and our mission to achieve economic growth and development.

I am sufficiently inspired by the examples of other successful diasporas to be convinced that this is a question to which we need to devote more thought and resources. Israel has achieved much of its political survival via its diaspora lobby in the US. The Philippines diaspora is more akin to Jamaica's, as most of their migrants leave for economic reasons, and remittances are a mainstay of the Philippine economy. The Philippine government's initiative with regard to its diaspora is to match overseas Filipino ventures, investors, and skills with domestic Filipino initiatives.

With a little ingenuity and some real participation from all the stakeholders – diaspora groups and NGOs, the government, and the businesses that serve the diaspora – into the whys, wherefores, and logistics, I think that a viable mechanism is within our reach in at least the medium term.

Notwithstanding the benefits of migration, I do have a concern about the fact that 85 per cent of our tertiary graduates migrate. I don't subscribe to the traditional 'brain drain' view, that skilled people migrating is a zero-sum game that ought be stopped. We can't hold people here if they don't perceive there are adequate opportunities for them. The most substantial way to reduce this mass migration of our skilled professionals is to provide the leadership and governance that create opportunities, or the atmosphere within which opportunities can be created, so that people will be encouraged to stay here and work.

If there aren't opportunities for them here, they are better off seeking greener pastures, and our immediate and more substantial challenge is to keep them connected and engaged.

What is problematic is that the majority of those graduates have been educated at taxpayers' expense, and it is unfair to all those people whose contributions made those graduates' education possible that they should migrate and leave Jamaican taxpayers holding the bag.

This is more an argument for a reform of the student loan system, together with a reexamination of the way that the government currently subsidizes The University of the West Indies and the University of Technology. Might it be more equitable to deposit the amount of the current subsidy into a low-interest need-blind loan pool and offer loans whose repayment is enforceable even if borrowers migrate? A positive step towards this end is the introduction of credit bureaus.

Migration, the diaspora, student loan policy – these are just a few of the many policy issues that we need to examine and re-think as we move towards Jamaica better fulfilling its development potential. These discrete concerns form a part of the bigger picture and context that all Jamaicans interested in the country's development must re-think and reformulate.

It was my wanting to play a more significant part in this bigger picture and the changes that need to take place that led me to re-engage in the political process virtually as soon as I landed back in Jamaica. I defended my thesis in June 2002 and returned to Jamaica shortly after with my doctorate under my belt, and a renewed sense of purpose. At that point, I didn't know precisely where I was heading, except that I was required to report back to UWI. And, too, politics beckoned. But I could not have anticipated the dramatic turn of events that awaited me back at home.

15

PRODIGAL SON

So much happened in such a short space of time when I got back to Jamaica in mid-2002. Within days of returning home with my family, I was involved in negotiating Bruce Golding's return to the Jamaica Labour Party (JLP). An election was due. There was immense pressure on Edward Seaga and the JLP from many different sectors of society to 'do something' to improve their prospects and prove themselves a viable opposition. The general consensus was that Bruce Golding was the JLP's only hope, and that Seaga and Golding had to reconcile their differences so that Golding could rejoin, re-enter, and save the JLP.

I had reached this same conclusion some time after the 2001 by-election in North East St Ann, and maintained it in the roughly two years since, that this was the most viable option at the time to present an alternative to the PNP, and that stood a chance of setting the country on the right path in the short and medium term.

But a good number of those who had stuck it out in the JLP were not so receptive to the idea. While many in the JLP, especially those who were senior members of the party, agreed that something needed to change, and that Seaga should step down, they were resistant to the idea of Bruce Golding returning and leapfrogging them to be party leader.

There were some who were pragmatic and recognized that, whether they liked Golding or not, he was the best option for the JLP to regain credibility and have a chance at returning to office. Thus Golding's return became a matter of expedience, a factor that would come back to haunt both Golding and the party.

Wayne Chen and I found ourselves among the negotiators between Golding and Seaga, and we went back and forth trying to broker an agreement. From our time with him in the National Democratic Movement (NDM), Golding was comfortable that we were committed to the NDM's Reform Agenda, and he trusted us that we had no personal ulterior motive in whether Golding went back to the JLP or not. Neither Wayne nor I stood to gain anything from the outcome; our only interest was in promoting what we considered the best way forward for Jamaica – not just for Golding or for the JLP.

The first stage of the negotiations was done in secret. When we went to meet with Seaga we had to go through a side door. He was not yet ready to make known that he was contemplating a rapprochement with Golding. I felt at the time that he deserved the time and space to do things his way and had no difficulty with the secrecy.

The challenge was similar within the NDM. There were former members of the NDM who felt completely betrayed by the entire arrangement. They felt that their time in the NDM had merely been a stepping stone for Golding to bide his time until Seaga was at the end of his tenure, and proof of that was their having been excluded from the consideration and negotiation of Golding's return.

That was not the case. Those people would never have agreed to Golding going back to the JLP. They had joined the NDM as an extension of their rejection of 'old-time' politics, which in their view was the modus operandi of the JLP. Their involvement in the negotiation of Golding's return to the JLP would have been futile and frustrating for everyone.

They were right, to an extent – the JLP had not changed since Golding had left. It was merely weaker for the exodus of many well-thinking Labourites to the NDM, or out of politics entirely, and Seaga was even weaker having lost yet another set of elections. I recognized that the party had stagnated, but I strongly believed that its rejuvenation was the only hope we had to break the stranglehold of the PNP over the country, and to move the country forward. The best prospects for that rebirth lay with the return of Bruce Golding.

Golding was under tremendous pressure, but he was reluctant to go back to the JLP. He felt that his credibility would be hampered by returning to the JLP, after all that had transpired since he had left the party seven years earlier, and the circumstances under which he had left.

Furthermore, Golding's convictions that the politics had to change remained. He was adamant that the JLP agree to adopt and pursue many of the policies and positions that had led him to leave in the first place – many of the positions that had been the foundation of the NDM. He would only agree to meeting with Seaga after Seaga had first conceded that he would entertain these proposals. Much of the work that Wayne and I, and others, did in our negotiations was around laying the groundwork for the crafting of what would later be called the JLP-Golding Memorandum of Understanding.

On September 26, 2002, Golding returned to the JLP, and its fortunes immediately improved. Though the JLP did not win the 2002 elections, held less than three weeks later, it showed much better than it would have, had Golding not returned. In any case, the funders would not have injected any money into the campaign were Golding not there – this was one of the key factors that pushed Seaga to take Golding back, the pressure from the donors. In his own memoir, *Edward Seaga: My Life and Leadership, Vol. 2, Hard Road to Travel, 1980-2008*, Seaga stated,

> I had not intended to invite Golding back into the party before the election as this would not be popular with the deputy leaders, some of whom saw themselves as a possible successor to me. They knew that Golding could pre-empt them all. I had planned to re-introduce him after the election because, notwithstanding all the double dealings against me in the 1990s enacted with or without his involvement, he was still the best bet for the future.
>
> In terms of his national profile, I had to think of the future of the party, not my own feelings. But with such a magnanimous offer of funding, I decided to advance the timetable. While it would be a turn-off to some, it would be a boost to me. So I agreed.

Had Golding gone back sooner, the JLP could have taken the election, but his re-entry had come too late.

I re-joined the JLP with Golding the same day. I was appointed to the JLP's Standing Committee and was involved in the immediate post-election discussion, which was centred around the question that everyone was asking: How do we rebuild the party to win the next time? Seaga's future as party leader came into sharp relief yet again.

Soon enough, Golding began to assume a leadership role in the party and was appointed to the Senate. For my part, I joined Generation 2000, otherwise called G2K, a relatively new JLP organization comprised of young professionals who sought to give the party greater focus on policy and winnability.

Little did I know that I was in for a year rife with drama and intrigue.

16

G2K

'G2K set to kick out Tufton', was the Sunday *Observer* front-page headline on July 6, 2003. The twists and turns of events that led to that point made for quite a saga.

I had now been back in Jamaica for just about a year, had jumped right into politics, and into the Jamaica Labour Party (JLP) on my return, and I was deeply enmeshed in the political process. I chose the G2K (Generation 2000) as my vehicle for participating in the JLP because it was the best fit for me at the time. David Panton, who was then a rising star in the JLP, had formed the organization in late 1999, together with other like-minded JLP supporters.

G2K considered itself the intellectual arm of the JLP, and its members were mostly university graduates who were not only book-smart but also engaged on the ground. It was a completely different organization from Young Jamaica, which at that time was floundering due to leadership issues and a series of unpleasant scandals.

The G2K's main objective was to provide policy and institutional support for the party, and to critically analyse the party's situation and future. I was appointed general secretary in November 2002 and elected president in October 2003. But not before a ridiculous series of events that even over a decade and a half later I find hard to believe actually happened.

As the *Observer* story had it, I was to be expelled for 'mischief-making', related to a handwritten, unsigned fax that was sent to local media houses. The fax alleged that there was a bitter war in the G2K between so-called Seaga loyalists and those who were thought to be Bruce Golding supporters, and that myself and other supposedly pro-Golding G2K members were being asked to resign as a result.

The idea was that the fax was seeking to publicize the issue and rally support for me and my colleagues by calling for a peaceful demonstration at the G2K executive meeting where our supposed expulsion was to take place. It was a convoluted story that was as preposterous as it sounded. I had nothing to do with any fax, and it was all a hoax.

But that headline and the incident were one in a series of such occurrences that had started when I joined the G2K six months before. In December 2002 another news story had alleged that there was a move afoot to 'dump' me as G2K General Secretary.

One of the things that I have come to learn about politics – and perhaps this is true of partisan politics around the world, not just Jamaica – is things are seldom what they seem. This was one of my first lessons in just how that functions. Even though the accusations – all of them – were untrue, they were indicative of the tensions that were most definitely present within the G2K and the JLP over my return.

There was a lot of intrigue within the JLP after Golding's re-entry and ascendance to leader, and in many ways that intrigue spilled over into G2K. The conventional wisdom was that I was Golding's proxy, while Norman Horne, who was then G2K's vice president and who was also vying for the presidency, was Seaga's. It followed that the supposed rift within the G2K was representative of the broader Seaga– Golding divisions within the party.

The perception was not entirely baseless. There were other happenings in the party that, if viewed from that perspective, could have led to such an assumption. The internal JLP race subsequent to the G2K contest, for the deputy leaders, saw those who were pro-leadership change defeat those who were considered pro-Seaga. James Robertson challenged Babsy Grange and won, and Horace Chang challenged Ed Bartlett and won. Robertson and Chang were not actually pro-Golding; it is more likely that they simply were in favour of a change in the party's leadership. But because of how the politics were then shaping up, their being pro-change-of-leadership led to the perception that they were anti-Seaga.

There did come a point, after having to deal with so much unnecessary drama, that I became discouraged and considered quitting G2K and abandoning my bid for the presidency. The stakes were high, as the G2K was considered, within the party and out, as one of the strongest, most cohesive, and most influential forces on the party and its future direction. And the future of the JLP was most certainly up for grabs at that point.

But once I shut out the noise, and focused on what was the right thing to do, I knew I could not quit. I turned inwards and knew that if I followed my own mind that I would do what was necessary to achieve my objectives, regardless of the obstacles being placed in front of me. I had the expectations of many other G2K members to live up to, and I could not let them down. Moreover, I wanted to clear my name of any wrongdoing related to all the rumours.

Most importantly, I was convinced that the G2K was an important organization. The G2K was playing a vital role in revitalizing the party's membership and ideas, and it was important not only for the JLP, but for Jamaican democracy, which was weakening as the JLP's strength had waned over the years. Once I made up my mind that I was going to proceed with my bid, I did so resolutely, and I refused to allow any of the shenanigans to affect me.

Seaga asked Arthur Williams, Jr. to preside over those elections, and the air was thick with tension. Despite the fax fiasco, I won the G2K presidential election against Horne, twelve votes to ten. The Jamaica *Observer* headline was 'Tufton Triumphs!' The media had itself contributed to the creation of the notion that the G2K contest was a proxy for the Seaga vs Golding saga, and they revelled in the ups and downs of what was happening.

This was my first real political victory, and even now perhaps the one in which the outcome was most uncertain – even more uncertain than the 2011 election. And yet the tension did not ease even though I had won. I suspected that Seaga was not pleased, a hunch that was strengthened when he called me in to convince me to make Horne, my opponent, general secretary.

I could not agree to his request. Having come out of such a contentious campaign, where so many attempts were made to undermine me and drag my name through the mud, to then appoint my former rival to the second most powerful position in the group was just not going to happen. I would be setting him up to subvert me and allow him to be Seaga's proxy after all. It was a matter of principle, regardless of what the media and others' perceptions were.

There was gridlock and inaction at the G2K for the next three months. Seaga appointed Abe Dabdoub – who was then still in the JLP though he defected to the PNP in 2006 – to mediate the discussions around the appointment of the executive, and continued, through Dabdoub, to advocate his preferences. I held out, and finally after three months I got the general secretary I wanted, Warren Newby. Both Norman Horne and his main ally in the G2K at the time, Ian Hayles, subsequently left the JLP and joined the PNP.

Once the hurdle of appointing the new G2K executive was cleared, the G2K continued to play an important role in the party. It is an attractive medium for young people to join the party. Over the years, it has grown into its intended role as the 'think tank' of the party, analysing and strategizing based on the empirical data from the many polls it has commissioned. They have carried out training exercises at all levels of the party.

Even though I have not played an active role in the G2K since the end of my presidency in 2005, I have continued to be involved. G2K was never intended to be a cheerleader for the JLP: it was committed to building the party, but not as a rubber stamp. The idea was that the G2K would be the conscience of the party, willing to take on controversial issues in an intellectually rigorous manner, even if it risked offending elements within the party, as long as it was in the party's best interests. The organization has had its ups and downs since then, which is the norm for any such body, and periodically it goes off track with some of its pronouncements and positions.

The G2K was at its weakest in the lead-up to and aftermath of the 2011 elections, when many, within and outside of the JLP, blamed them for the party's humiliating defeat. Again, the truism that things are not what they seem comes to the fore; there was so much more than what the G2K did or didn't do that amounted to that outcome. But I jump ahead. In the 2007 election campaign, the G2K was instrumental in the JLP's victory, when I took the seat of South West St Elizabeth out of the clutches of the PNP after 18 years. My early experiences in the G2K, it would turn out, were a microcosm of my position in the JLP and foreshadowed similar dramas yet to come.

17

BROWN MAN CURSE

In the Jamaican classification scheme of skin colour I am either a red man or a brown man. Both designations come with packages of meanings, consensually held by most Jamaicans, mainly regarding socio-economic status and geographical origin. I had been hearing I was 'red' since I was a boy, but I had never attached much importance to it, and I wasn't conscious of my skin colour having any particular significance for me, until I entered politics.

Politics is the one arena where I can say without fear of contradiction that my skin colour has had an effect – and where I can definitively point to it being a disadvantage. Not so much in the National Democratic Movement (NDM), but certainly in the Jamaica Labour Party (JLP), my 'brownness' has constantly been a problematic issue. In my view and experience, and though many might disagree, I consider that it is more of a disadvantage to be brown-skinned than an advantage in the modern Jamaican political arena.

In some parts of Jamaica, such as in upper St Andrew neighbourhoods and in communities where there was a strong presence of light-brown peasant farmers, they used to say that the browner man would win the seat. I don't know if anyone has ever actually tested this proposition, but in today's Jamaica 'brownness' is no longer a guarantee of political success.

If it ever was true, since the 1970s and in post-Michael Manley Jamaican politics, and particularly since the era of P.J. Patterson's leadership of the People's National Party (PNP) and his time as prime minister, it has become unfashionable to be white or fair-skinned in Jamaican politics. All things being equal – charisma, ability, likeability, campaign success – I would argue that the darker brown-skinned candidate has an advantage over the lighter-skinned candidate in any political contest in Jamaica today. And indeed I can think of a few white or near-white Jamaicans who would be interested in entering the political arena but whose skin colour dampens their viability, as well as some who are already in politics but whose rise beyond a certain leadership level is stymied for the same reason.

In a country such as Jamaica, where the majority of people are dark-skinned and where there is a history of white colonialism and, some would argue, 'brown neocolonialism', it is normal and expected that people should want their political representatives and leaders to look like them. The assumption, whether true or not, is that such a similarity will mean that they will represent their interests. That was certainly the implication of P.J. Patterson's assertion during the 1997 election campaign that he could easily leave the platform of a political meeting to mingle with the crowd and no one would be able to tell him apart from the people around him; a statement which stands as a significant crucible in the complex dynamics of race and politics in Jamaica.

Just as I suspected happened at UWI, even though I was a fatherless lower-middle-class boy from Manchester, in politics the first thing that people see is my complexion, and they make assumptions about who I am and where I come from on that basis. In many ways, I embody the typical

Jamaican success story – born in humble circumstances to a single mother but moved upward due to education and hard work – but most Jamaican people probably do not see themselves in me. Knowing that I am not a St Elizabeth red man, my skin colour creates the impression of someone who was born into privilege.

My political opponents know this well and use it – a perverse iteration of the race card – every chance they get. The untrue stories that circulate about my supposed privileged background would be hilarious, except that people actually believe the lies.

Especially now that I have a doctorate and have had a public profile for so many years, the assumption that I am from a privileged upper-middle-class background has become more apocryphal. The irony is that the people who seek to use this against me are the ones who know that it is untrue.

As someone who is very open about my background, it is easy for me to forget that people don't know that the colour of my skin really has nothing to do with where I am coming from and who I am as a person. But it has come up so many times that I have accepted that this is something I will always have to deal with. In politics, your opponents and detractors will use whatever ammunition they have to try to discredit and undermine you.

Because I don't come from the privileged family background that people assume, I sometimes find it difficult to muster up the energy to battle the constant misperceptions about me, and to fight those who try to use the colour of my skin as a political weapon against me. Perhaps if I were a son of privilege, I might consider it worthwhile to defend myself. I might have some Jamaican version of liberal guilt that would motivate me to work at proving myself, and which would energize me to combat the misperception.

But I am not a son of privilege, not by any measure, nor have I had any favours granted me because of my skin colour. I should not have to prove that I am 'not really brown' to anyone, and it is difficult for me to do so, because exactly what is it that I am supposed to be trying to prove? And while I understand why skin colour is an issue in Jamaica, and why people try to use it against me, my heart is just not in that fight.

It is like someone accusing you of committing a crime but you don't know what the crime is. You know you are innocent, but you have to defend yourself so that the accusation doesn't stick. But it takes its toll, this constant defensiveness about something that I don't really believe is worth the energy it consumes, while at the same time I am present to the fact that skin colour is a problematic reality for many Jamaicans.

In a paradoxical and complicated way – as issues regarding race, colour, and class are – I suppose I am privileged, to not be subject to what can be characterized as the 'anti-privilege' of being dark-skinned in Jamaica. For all my supposed trials and tribulations, there are many who have unfairly and continuously been put at a disadvantage in one way or another in far worse circumstances than I ever have.

I look forward to the day when skin colour is not an issue for anyone, when people are measured by their actions and their character. Jamaica has come a long way in these matters, but I doubt if these types of issues will ever disappear completely.

I have had to learn how to cope with the unpredictability of people's perceptions and, especially in politics, the extremes to which people will go to undermine and weaken their opponents. The colour of my skin was not the only issue that was weaponized against me. From the outset, and for years thereafter, I was bedevilled by my association with Bruce Golding. A great deal of the suspiciousness and resentment over Golding's return to the JLP was projected onto me. The reality of my relationship with Golding was far from straightforward, however. Indeed, it was replete with its own paradoxes and contradictions.

18

GOLDING

Regardless of his missteps, and no matter what his fiercest detractors may say, Bruce Golding is one of Jamaica's greatest politicians, and his contributions to Jamaica's political and democratic development will be recognized, if not now, then in years to come, as critical junctures, for both good and bad.

As a political orator he is unparalleled in modern Jamaican politics. I can think of few other politicians, anywhere, with his ability to analyse and explain complex issues. Even when he has taken positions that I disagreed with, I have marvelled at his ability to construct an argument and come up with answers and solutions that, all together, seem perfectly sound.

His victory speech on September 3, 2007, when the Jamaica Labour Party (JLP) finally won an election for the first time since 1980, together with the speech at his swearing-in as prime minister eight days later, should go down as required reading for all students of Jamaican political history, as should many of the speeches he gave during the formation and early days of the National Democratic Movement (NDM).

I have been seen, since my time in the NDM and through to his resignation in 2011, as a 'Golding-ite', even more than as a Labourite. The assumption was reasonable, on the face of it. I had been a founding member of the NDM, with Golding. I had returned to the JLP with Golding, and I had played an important role in advocating and negotiating that return. But Golding did not influence my participation in the JLP, particularly my early activity within the G2K and my aspiration for the G2K presidency, in any way. Once the JLP got into office in 2007, my interactions with him attenuated gradually but significantly.

But the association, regardless of how much the perception reflected or diverged from the truth, has been with me throughout my political career. In the case of the G2K, while Norman Horne was very much Seaga's pick, Golding had outright discouraged me from running for the G2K presidency. I suppose – and I use the word suppose deliberately because we actually did not talk about this – Golding felt that, given the assumption that I was his proxy (though I was not), if I were to lose my bid, it would weaken him, and send a message that Seaga still wielded power.

Another misperception that people seem to have had over the years is that I had influence over Golding. Bruce Golding is an extremely private person and quite impermeable to influence from others. There are only a handful of instances in which it could be suggested that I had any sway on any decision he made.

Golding didn't have the proverbial 'kitchen cabinet' – a small group of people who he regularly turned to for advice and guidance, and who influenced his decisions – that most politicians are thought to have. He has sought others' opinions from time to time, as would be natural, but from what I know of him, most of his decisions have been arrived at after he has carefully studied and considered the variables in question. If his decision is in accordance with others' advice or opinions, it is probably that his views coincided with theirs, and not that they led him to their position.

Yes, he had close friends, but I would not conclude that they were able to unduly influence his decision making, particularly after he made his mind up on a matter. One could even say that Golding is somewhat of a loner, a posture that has brought him mixed results.

I supported Bruce Golding's vision and principles in the NDM, his return to the JLP, and once in the JLP, I supported most of his positions there, particularly in the campaign and at the outset of his time in office. After our time in the NDM had run its course, it was through working with him that I got my first appointment to political office as he selected me to replace him in the Senate when he became JLP leader. For all I have learnt from him, and for all the political doors that he opened for me, I am grateful.

But there has been a downside and the G2K 'cass-cass' was just my first taste of this. Especially among some senior people in the JLP, I have often been viewed with suspicion and distrust because of my association with Golding. My quick rise within the JLP – which is only remarkable because the JLP, like the PNP, is a party whose hierarchy is determined by longevity and dues-paying, not necessarily meritocratic achievement or potential for carrying the party forward – has generated controversy that has dogged me and my political journey. Some within the party have resented my rise and have asserted, both overtly and implicitly, that I rode on Golding's coat-tails and, thus, I have not deserved the positions in the party that I have occupied.

Another drawback to being linked to Golding has been, as the Jamaican saying goes, 'if you can't catch Kwaku, catch him shut' (meaning: if you can't get what you are after, get the next closest thing). Those who had a beef with Golding often let that either spill over onto me, or they would target me directly, in lieu of going after Golding.

Since I re-entered the JLP, I have worked tirelessly within the party, at many different levels – in the G2K, in the constituency, with the delegates, in the executive and at the national level – to represent and build the party, and I have done that as my own person, not as an agent or representative of anyone else. I do these things because I believe that the JLP represents the best possibility for Jamaica to move forward.

Yet, this perception of my closeness to Golding and the dynamic that it has created has served to distract and frustrate when I am forced to deal with issues that are rooted in pointless mischief. More importantly, it has been a counterproductive distraction to the party, where the time and energy spent dealing with conspiracies against me would be much better spent building and uniting the party.

This is not to say that my efforts have been in vain. Regardless of their perceptions and possible suspicions when I first re-joined the JLP, the party delegates have repeatedly indicated that they have long since moved beyond that. That was unequivocally proven by my 2010 election to the position of deputy leader, which is a selection based on the delegates' votes. The base of the party accepted me and what I represented, regardless of my previous association with the NDM, or Golding, and they trusted me to carry their and the party's interests forward.

My motivation upon entering national politics, first in the NDM, and once I re-entered the JLP, has always been to promote the concerns of Jamaicans and to work towards national development. I have worked to appeal to people – my constituents in South West St Elizabeth, then in West Central St Catherine, and the broader Jamaican electorate – as well as to the delegates, as they are the first point of contact between the people and the politician, so that they will trust me to carry out their mandate.

In a broader sense, my constituency is all Jamaicans who hopefully see me as someone who they can work with to move the country forward. I will do this whether I am in the JLP or outside of Jamaican party politics. I have maintained this position, as reflected in my decisions in 2013 and 2014 to retreat from active involvement in the JLP, and my decision in 2015 to re-insert myself in a more direct way.

The vicissitudes of my association with Golding have been yet another aspect of my journey in Jamaican politics. There has never been a dull moment, either at the national level or at the internal party level, whether in office or in opposition. The antics of the G2K were but a taste of what was to come – the first twist on the roller coaster of my time in Jamaican politics. I got a fuller dose of the ups and downs of holding a national office when Golding appointed me to the Senate.

19

SENATE, ROUND ONE

I was appointed an opposition senator on June 24, 2005, filling the vacancy left by Bruce Golding. Earlier that year, in February, Seaga had finally stepped down from the leadership of the Jamaica Labour Party (JLP). He was the second-longest serving head of a political movement in the Western hemisphere when he did so. (Paraguay's dictator Alfredo Stroessner held the record.)

Golding assumed leadership of the JLP, and shortly thereafter became a Member of Parliament (MP), having won the by-election for Seaga's West Kingston seat. Having returned to the JLP with Golding, and given my association with him, it could be seen that this was political reward for having been a faithful foot soldier. That is nothing unusual in the way that Jamaican Senate appointments are made. Regardless, I would like to think that being selected represented Golding's good judgment about my capacity to make a worthwhile contribution in the House. That was certainly my intention on being appointed.

This was my first official national appointment. Though I had a national profile from my participation in the National Democratic Movement (NDM), I was now holding a state position. The official function of the Senate, also called the Upper House, is as a chamber of review. What this means, according to its original intentions when established in the early 1960s, is that there would always be enough opposition members (13 of the 21 senators are appointed by the ruling party and eight by the opposition) so that any proposed constitutional change would have to be negotiated between the ruling party and the opposition.

Though on a day-to-day basis we might not see the Senate 'doing' anything that seems particularly significant, the Senate's existence is an important safeguard to the Constitution. So far it has not happened that the Senate has had to step in to block a drastic move to change the Constitution, but it is important for our democracy that such a mechanism exists.

The Senate also ensures that regardless of the parliamentary majority held by the ruling party, another legislative body exists that guarantees the opposition some voice in the making and modifying of the country's laws. This was important during the 1980s when the People's National Party (PNP) boycotted the 1983 election and the Parliament was dominated completely by the JLP.

The members of the Senate are generally political appointments, though there have been senators appointed as 'independent' in the past. A Senate appointment is also a way for a ruling party to access a broader selection of possible persons to appoint as cabinet ministers.

For both parties a Senate appointment confers recognition that this person is valued by the party for his past, present, or potential contribution to the party and the country. Though it is time-consuming – between attending sittings of the Senate every Friday and preparing for the debates – and it is virtually unpaid (there is a tiny stipend), it is an honour to be able to serve one's country in such an official capacity.

My focus during my tenure as a senator was, probably predictably, on the broad questions of Jamaica's failure to realize its economic development potential and the political context of Jamaica's dismal development path. These had been my concerns from my early political awakening, as they likely are for anyone motivated to serve. I called for a reform agenda, along the lines of what the NDM had been calling for and what Bruce Golding was making the effort to incorporate in the Labour Party's positions now that he was leader.

Of particular concern was the quality of local representation and the role of the MP. Even though I was yet to experience being an MP, I had heard enough complaints by citizens and done enough research at the time to conclude that Jamaicans were just not satisfied with their local political representation. I was keen on trying to improve this and recommended, among other things, a government-supported Office of the Member of Parliament for MPs to be present for a minimum time period each week to serve the entire constituency, not just those who voted for him/her.

I also advocated for MPs developing a five-year development plan for their constituency, after consultation with stakeholder groups in their local areas. It would have given greater weight to citizen participation, which would be a step in the direction of a healthier political culture. Citizens would realize that there are collective projects that they can benefit from and that patronage does not have to be the order of the day. These were not original ideas, but I felt that they could go a long way in improving the visibility and effectiveness of MPs. It would also give constituents an opportunity to assess their MP's performance in a more objective way for future elections.

I was also concerned about Jamaica's young people, and the hopelessness and lack of preparedness that too many youth suffer from, and the fact that the 16–30 age group dominates Jamaica's prison population. A direct cause of this, and another issue that I raised in the Senate, was the unemployment rate and the difficulty for people, especially young people, to find jobs. Again, not the first time that these issues were being raised, but nevertheless problems that I wanted us to find solutions for.

I raised concerns about how the Ministry of Education was reporting the CXC exam results. They were using the statistics to paint a much rosier picture than really obtained. Having since been in office myself, I better understand the balancing act that a minister has to walk between being honest and forthcoming, and not delivering bad news all the time. It is a challenge of governance, broadly speaking, that bedevils all of us.

Tourism is Jamaica's biggest opportunity for moving forward. My analysis of the industry indicated that we needed improvements on three fronts. First, we need to retain in Jamaica a larger proportion of each dollar spent. Second, we need to magnify the multiplier effect of tourism, by more efficiently linking the tourism industry to other local enterprises such as transportation, food services, entertainment, and manufacturing. Third, greater efforts are to be expended in increasing the amount of money each tourist spends while vacationing in Jamaica.

The data at that time showed that of every dollar spent on tourism in Jamaica, only half was retained, while the rest went out of the country. The big challenge was how to increase the retention rate, the immediate effect of which would be greater support for more local economic activity, and the benefits that would be derived to the local economy. To realize the full potential of the tourism industry, an effective linkage programme had to be developed to ensure that each tourist spent most of their vacation budget on local activities and products.

As with all the other experiences in my life, I approached my first Senate appointment not only as a job to be done, but as a learning opportunity, in this case into how policy issues were raised and addressed. Many of the issues that I sought to address through the Senate are still with us – unemployment, hopelessness, unsatisfactory performance of the economy, lagging educational outcomes, failure to maximize tourism's full developmental potential. What I began to realize then and have learned since is that it takes a tremendous amount of work, resources, cooperation and will, to effect change in Jamaica. There is also the matter of timing within the political cycle and the limited time span in which things can be done. With an election every four to four and a half years, if you give six months to settle into a portfolio, you then have two and a half years to try to accomplish anything before the country switches gear to election mode. Big ideas, big reforms, big changes usually need more time than that.

I saw that the Senate can and ought to be strengthened. I saw this my first time as a Senator, and I recognized the same weaknesses in my second time around as an opposition senator (2011–13/2015–16). There are strengths: though senators are politically appointed, the discourse and debate tend to transcend partisan bickering, which is a positive aspect of the Senate. There are exceptions to this, largely based on the personalities of senators, but for the most part it is a collegial group.

However, there is a need for more technical support by way of research assistance and education, and training on the issues for senators, so they have greater capacity to contribute to the debates and decisions on issues of national concern. I had the advantage of my academic background, so data-driven analysis was second nature to me. I had also been exposed to many of the issues over the course of so many years of studying development-related topics.

In my second senate appointment, I was in a position to contribute more because my time in government had given me a better understanding of how the legislative process works, how the political cycle works, and what some of the country's real needs were. I raised more specific issues like making the business environment more efficient, internationalization of business and the protection of intellectual property, modernizing agriculture, and the need to legislate rainwater harvesting as an important response to climate change and poor infrastructure.

Senators without government experience should be given the training and preparation that will allow them to make more informed and useful contributions to the debate than what obtains at present. There is a need to re-examine the research support senators, and legislators in general, receive as they seek to carry out their duties to the Jamaican people. There needs to be far greater emphasis on data collection and analysis so that decisions are made based on reality and not on what a person 'thinks' or 'feels'. Otherwise, we run the risk of passing bad laws due to ignorance.

In Golding's first speech as JLP party leader in February 2005, he made it clear that once P.J. Patterson stepped down, which he had signalled he would, Golding would be moving the party into election mode. So said, so done. My time in the Senate turned out to be short-lived.

Not even a year after my senate appointment, in March 2006, Portia Simpson Miller became prime minister, and the Jamaican political climate took on a sense of urgency as we all began to anticipate an election with two new leaders at the helms of the respective parties. By mid-2006, both parties were gearing up for a poll that was due in at least a year, and everything began to move at breakneck speed. I was in the midst of it all, preparing myself for the next big race.

20

St Elizabeth
South West

After the 2002 elections, I identified the seat of South West St Elizabeth as a possibility, should I decide to participate in representational politics. Seaga and others in the Jamaica Labour Party (JLP) had long thought I would be a good fit for the Central Manchester constituency, as they considered me to have a 'middle class' profile. Ironic, given that I was not a product of the Mandeville middle class, even though I was born and raised in the area, but typical of the misperceptions people have long held based on my skin colour and their automatic assumption of where I 'fit' in Jamaica's complicated social and colour class dynamics.

I felt more comfortable in SW St Elizabeth. An added attraction for me was that my wife Neadene is from the area, and I had long ago fallen in love with the beautiful towns of Black River and Treasure Beach, and was generally enamoured with the constituency, its people, and its potential.

Comprising 155 square miles, with 40,000 inhabitants and about 23,000 voters, the constituency of SW St Elizabeth was considered a swing seat, although dominated by the People's National Party (PNP) for the previous two decades. Derrick Sangster had won it for the JLP in 1980, but since 1989 the seat had been won by a wide margin by the PNP candidate and stalwart Comrade, Donald 'Danny' Buchanan.

After 2002, Sangster stepped down as JLP candidate-caretaker, and I vied for the caretaker position against Keith Reynolds, a local businessman from a prominent family with roots in the area. Buchanan was set to retire from active politics, and churchman and educator Stanley Redwood had taken over from him as the PNP's caretaker-candidate.

At my first attempt I won the seat handily, by 1,825 votes. My second time around I lost the seat by 13 votes. Neither my victory nor my loss can be understood without delving into the fundamental structure – and weaknesses – of Jamaican electoral politics.

I was intrigued by the town of Black River, its history, its geography, its biodiversity, and its potential. Black River was the first place in Jamaica to get electricity. The Black River is the longest navigable river in Jamaica and a major source of economic activity for locals, and the town of Black River is the only one in Jamaica where an active river is a central feature of the town.

The other areas of the constituency are equally interesting. The Pedro Plains and its environs are among the most fertile in Jamaica, where the majority of people are engaged in farming, small-scale commerce, fishing, or tourism. Farmers work extremely hard to provide critical short-term crops like vegetables and seasonings for the entire country, hence the reputation of the area as the 'bread basket' of Jamaica. The area's farmers are credited with mastering the art of 'dry farming', a technique used to retain moisture in the soil by covering it with a carpet of dried grass.

The constituency contains a wide expanse of Jamaica's south coast, and tourism and fishing are as important as agriculture. Fisherfolk there learn their trade primarily as apprentices, and community tourism is characterized by small roadside shops offering a range of local products like soups, jerk pork and chicken, watermelon and, of course, rum. All of this makes for a rich heritage that is rooted in the area people's traditions and culture.

Treasure Beach thrives in its own unique way, a way that can and ought to be replicated in other areas of the island. The people of Treasure Beach have developed and sustained low-impact, community-oriented tourism that has brought previously unknown prosperity to the area and can serve as a model for the rest of Jamaica and, indeed, the Caribbean.

On the eastern side of the constituency, fishing, farming, and small-scale commerce are the main forms of economic activity. The town of Middle Quarters is home to Jamaica's hot peppered shrimp, and is a popular stop for Jamaicans and foreign tourists.

As I came to know and understand the constituency better, I came to respect the people of the area for their independence and tenacity. Perhaps that is true of many other Jamaicans in other parts of the island, but the work that the farmers, fisherfolk, and tourism workers do throughout the parish of St Elizabeth, despite the poor roads, limited access to water, and weak infrastructure, gives real meaning to the notion of Jamaican resilience and enterprise.

The parish on a whole, like the rest of Jamaica, has too many people living below the poverty line, and the educational attainment levels are dismal. Only about half of the people of the parish have access to piped water, and only 20 per cent to indoor taps. In the twenty-first century this is unacceptable.

My victory in 2007 effectively wrested the constituency from the PNP's 18-year stranglehold. How I did it was neither revolutionary nor innovative. I simply became a master of the game of Jamaican representational politics. In the two years prior to the 2007 elections, I travelled from Kingston, where I lived and worked at UWI, to the constituency three to four times a week.

I was able to spend a lot of time there because of the flexibility of my teaching schedule, and I could stay with my in-laws if I overnighted. One semester, Derrick Deslandes, who coordinated the marketing programme in the Department of Management Studies, and I arranged for Damion Crawford to come on as an adjunct lecturer to teach my class Principles of Marketing, so I could have more time to spend in the constituency. Damion had been a Guild of Undergraduates president, and was retracing the footsteps of many of his predecessors going from the UWI Guild to active party politics, where he headed the PNP Youth Organization (PNPYO) for two terms. (He went on to become PNP Member of Parliament for St Andrew East Rural, 2011–2016, and was elected PNP vice-president in 2018.) I was everywhere – at every funeral, community gathering, and school prize-giving. People must have thought I had cloned myself, the way they saw me so often. I did nothing extraordinary. I simply followed the campaign playbook to the letter. This is where having a regular family life – dinner with your wife, helping the children with homework – is impossible. If you want to have a chance at winning, this is what you have to do.

The national picture and the general leaning of the electorate away from the PNP and toward the JLP augmented my personal efforts. SW St Elizabeth has to date consistently demonstrated the characteristics of a weather vane seat, going with the winning party in nearly every election ever held in Jamaica, and in 2007, I was part of a winning campaign.

Golding, having returned to the JLP, did an excellent job in uniting the party, if for nothing else but to win the 2007 election. His ascension to party leader was not seamless, but he emerged in time and convincingly enough to successfully steer the party to victory.

He dedicated himself completely to the campaign. Perhaps he saw that he had to vindicate himself in the eyes of the skeptics within the JLP as to his value to the party, and also to those Jamaicans who saw his return to the JLP as a pointless venture. He virtually lived on the road, mobilizing the party's base, and energizing the delegates with his vision.

In addition to the JLP faithful, Golding brought with him some of the undecided/uncommitted voters who had been attracted to, or participated in, the National Democratic Movement (NDM), and together with nudging the JLP hardcore out of apathy and getting them out on Election Day, we managed to win the election by a hair's breadth – 32 to 28.

At the same time, regardless of Golding's work and commitment, he could not have done it without the thousands of party workers – delegates and polling division workers especially – who contributed to the effort.

At the leadership level of the party, it is certain that without the work of the Generation 2000 (G2K) we would likely not have won the election. Personalities like Daryl Vaz brought a lot of energy to the campaign. Marissa Dalrymple-Philbert was a strong campaigner who did the work. Veterans like Mike Henry, Horace Chang, Desmond McKenzie, Karl Samuda, Pearnel Charles, Ed Bartlett, Audley Shaw, James Robertson and Robert 'Bobby' Montague, together with relative newcomers like Michael Stern, Warren Newby, Ian Murray, and Gregory Mair, went all out in contributing to the effort.

Local government representatives – councillors and councillor-caretakers – also played significant roles in organizing and working for the party at the local level. Oftentimes we forget their contribution but they are the ones who live among the people and understand their concerns and are fastest in responding to those concerns. They were critical to the JLP's efforts.

It was no lovefest. Golding's re-entry into the party created a lot of animosity. But he demonstrated the capacity to reach out to those who considered him their enemy, and they responded. There was a determination of all concerned that the singular focus was getting the PNP out of office. People were prepared to overlook their bitterness and resentment about Golding's re-entry towards that goal. It is that unity of purpose that contributed significantly to the JLP victory in 2007, and candidates like myself in marginal seats like SW St Elizabeth being brought home comfortably.

Despite this ostensible oneness, the fundamental fractures and weaknesses were still there in the party, and the unity proved to be transitory. None of this – the underlying tensions nor the impermanence of the solidarity that won the party the election – was adequately dealt with after the election victory. This would prove to be to our detriment later.

My victory in SW St Elizabeth was also attributed, at least in part, to the fatigue the country felt with the PNP. The national mood was decidedly discontented with the PNP, especially at the local level – the daily challenges of poor roads, inadequate water supply, and deteriorating or insufficient infrastructure had worn down people's trust in the PNP. Even for the PNP die-hearted there was a frustration with the lack of tangible progress after such a long time in office, and many of the PNP core did not turn out to shore up support for their party.

This fundamental dynamic in Jamaican electoral politics is crucial to understanding any election. Jamaican elections are won or lost depending on the extent to which either party is able to mobilize its core support *and* garner a proportion of uncommitted voters. In 2007, the JLP had its loyalists turn out and enough – not a majority, not even a large proportion, but enough – of the uncommitted voted for them. The PNP base, on the other hand, did not turn out in full force and they did not appeal to the uncommitted at all in 2007.

This was proven in 2011 when the uncommitted did not come out, and the PNP base was sufficiently mobilized and outnumbered the JLP base, which was not adequately mobilized. Again in 2016, the PNP base stayed home, the JLP base came out, and the uncommitted showed up just enough for the JLP to eke out a victory.

Despite the PNP fatigue and the energy that Golding brought to the campaign in 2007, the JLP faced a formidable opponent in Portia Simpson Miller. She was new to the party's leadership, a strong populist and very popular among the Jamaican people. She has an enviable connection with people that few Jamaican politicians can claim, and regardless of what one might think about her policies and her record, no one can deny her charismatic appeal to many Jamaicans, as she proved time and time again.

Election night September 2007 was bittersweet. Though it was clear from the early returns that I would win, one of my workers, Muir, was attacked and badly hurt that night. He was parking his car at the Black River courthouse when someone slashed his throat and he had to be rushed to the Black River Hospital. He was diabetic and was in a serious crisis. Fortunately, he recovered, but I was in the police station making a report about the attempted murder on my worker when I was declared a winner. I felt cheated of the opportunity to savour my victory, yet conflicted that I was feeling that way when a loyal party worker – one who had helped secure that victory – was battling for his life.

When I left Muir in the hospital, his outcome still uncertain, I went back to the constituency office to greet my supporters. I gave a speech, but I was disheartened and concerned for Muir's welfare.

The next morning I woke up to pans banging outside my gate. Thousands of people were in the streets. I got word that Muir was on the path to full recovery. The police called me to come out and address the crowd to get them to disperse as there was chaos and havoc through the town. I had to literally lead the crowd out in a motorcade. We drove through the entire constituency and ended in Mountain Side Square. By the time we arrived it was just turning to dusk, and a full sound system was in place. Mannish water and curry goat were on the fire, and white rum flowed into the wee hours of the next morning.

Despite the marginal seat count victory at the national level, I was never in any doubt that the JLP would win that election. I had won my seat by an extremely comfortable margin, though that victory did not come easy. But a disturbing thing happened that night: Portia Simpson Miller did not concede the PNP's loss, and she never did subsequently. In his victory speech, Golding went to lengths to encourage JLP supporters to remain calm, and Simpson Miller did not say anything inflammatory enough to mobilize disgruntled PNP supporters, so the potential for unrest was fortunately quelled. There were people who suspected this would happen, who warned senior people in the PNP that this was a possibility; whether they acted to forestall it, and their efforts were in vain, I don't know. Most people assumed that when she didn't concede that night, she would do so the next morning, yet she remained steadfast. The English-speaking Caribbean and especially Jamaica is characterized by stable democracies, and one of the most important features of a stable democracy is that the loser concedes immediately. Jamaica has maintained this tradition faithfully since Universal Adult Suffrage. Her refusal to do what tradition required brought into question Simpson Miller's own commitment to democracy. It was topical for a few days after the election, and then it faded from public discussion. The question remains though: what was she thinking? That she was above the rules and norms? That given all the other barriers she had broken through to get to be Jamaica's first female prime minister, she was not beholden to the status quo? Simpson Miller was never sanctioned for it, and she went on to lead the PNP for another ten years, including serving another term as prime minister.

The ups and downs of the campaign, the drama on election night, and the initial uncertainty of the outcome of the election itself were nothing, however, compared to the rough road that lay ahead.

21

MP

The type of campaigning activity that got me elected to the Parliament in 2007 is only possible when a candidate is in opposition, or if one is on the backbench, unless it is a garrison constituency where votes are virtually guaranteed regardless of what the candidate does. Once you are an elected Member of Parliament (MP) and especially if you are a member of the Cabinet, and, even more so, if you take your cabinet position seriously and want to make something of a record for yourself and your time in office, it is impossible to be present in the way that your constituents want and have come to expect. This is particularly so when you are MP for a seat that is located a fair distance from Kingston.

This is exactly what happened once I had won the seat of SW St Elizabeth and was appointed to the Cabinet. I took my job at the Ministry of Agriculture, and later at the Ministry of Industry and Commerce, very seriously, and threw myself into my work. I still went to the constituency at least once a week, but between the overseas travel and the obligations that kept me in Kingston where the Parliament and the Ministry are located, I had nowhere near the visibility that I had built up prior to 2007.

I had a strong team of people representing me in the constituency and we managed to fulfil nearly all of the promises made during the campaign. Using resources from the Constituency Development Fund (CDF) together with ongoing fund-raising from private sector donors, we resurfaced roads, installed fences at schools and playfields, and implemented the Rural Electrification Programme which brought electricity to some remote places. We sponsored and organized sporting activities and competitions, and constructed and refurbished changing rooms at sports complexes.

The most important achievements were in developing infrastructure in the area for people to improve the gains from their livelihood, which in SW St Elizabeth are fishing and farming. We rehabilitated a small ruminant (goats and sheep) training facility in Hounslow, constructed a vegetable packing house together with GraceKennedy, and built a peppermash factory to purchase hot peppers from farmers to produce hot pepper sauce and other value-added pepper products.

I was determined to construct a new market in Black River as the existing facility was dilapidated and unsanitary. This was a project that was long overdue. It was a travesty, the market that existed. But the cost of a new market was tremendous. The government alone could not stand the cost, though to be fair it was never a government initiative per se, it was more a personal commitment I had made in my manifesto as candidate.

It took a major project management approach, bringing together a number of government agencies and a few private companies who gave their time and work at no charge. I put in whatever I could of the constituency's CDF funds, and we obtained a major contribution from a private sector donor.

We broke ground in October 2011, and the construction of a new market commenced. But it would be up to the PNP government to complete the project, however, as the elections came just two months later, well before it was completed. I lost the seat, and it was up to the new MP to take it over.

Another priority during my time in office was to improve the education infrastructure in the constituency's schools, and to help children and parents increase their and their children's educational attainment. I met with school principals and spent a lot of time designing projects and raising money to support the build out of educational institutions.

We didn't achieve all of our goals, but we built a computer lab at the Black River Primary School and equipped it with 40 computers, and we saw to the construction of two new basic schools in the community of Slipe. We implemented improvement projects for many other educational institutions and supported hundreds of students at all levels of education with back to school support each year.

For the fisherfolk we repaired and refurbished the facilities, including the bathrooms, at the Great Bay Fishing Beach. At Calabash Bay, gear sheds were constructed as well as at other fishing beaches. A fish sanctuary was established, and more extension officers were assigned to the area, for both agriculture and fisheries.

Even though I wasn't physically in the constituency as I had been while campaigning, the planning and mobilizing and implementing of projects and programmes never ceased, and I always tried to provide the necessary leadership.

Then I was transferred to a new and challenging ministry, the Ministry of Industry and Commerce, just five months before the election. I was again determined to effect some positive change there. This was an area that I had a great deal of interest in – my studies had been perfect preparation for the role – and I had a lot of ideas that I was excited about bringing to fruition. I had not yet absorbed the timing of the political cycle, where anything significant has to be done in the first two and a half years of an administration's term, and I certainly didn't expect to be contesting an election so soon after being installed in that ministry. In the critical months prior to the election, I was not on the ground in the constituency as I would have had to be, if I wanted to guarantee retaining the seat.

The fact that I was not re-elected to the seat in 2011 was not, in my mind, a reflection of my performance as an MP with regard to the work I did for the constituency. I am confident that the lives of the people of SW St Elizabeth were improved because of my work during my tenure, and that people benefited from the programmes I introduced and the infrastructure that was installed between 2007 and 2011. I stand by my record as MP for that constituency, and am proud of the work that my team and I did.

I wanted to win the seat and was disappointed when I lost; indeed, I was disappointed that the JLP lost the election. The work in the constituency aside, the Bruce Golding-led Cabinet worked tremendously hard in our respective ministries.

This was not enough to give us a victory, however. I learned from that experience that work alone is not enough for political success – it is how the electorate perceives you, and very literally, if they see you. At the constituency level, visibility is critical, and as much as the work was being done, I personally was not on the ground enough for people to see me. I was not at the prize-givings, the dead yards, and the football matches.

At the national level perception was also crucial. Despite our gains as an administration, the electorate perceived us as arrogant and uncaring, and we failed to communicate our achievements in a way that was accessible to voters. But it wasn't our perceived arrogance or lack of caring that lost us the 2011 election. There was far more to the story.

22

LOCKED IN THE CABINET

The Cabinet is the highest decision-making body in Jamaica. Based on our constitution and the Whitehall–Westminster system of parliamentary democracy that we practice, it is the principal policy arm of the government. The Prime Minister and the Cabinet's role is to guide government policy.

Cabinet meets weekly (there are also special meetings that can be held at any time, in addition to the regular weekly meeting), and is chaired by the Prime Minister. Every Cabinet member signs an oath of secrecy – nothing that happens in Cabinet is ever to be discussed outside of Cabinet; it is a commitment that is taken very seriously in Jamaica, which is why on the rare occasions that there is a leak, it is newsworthy.

The Whitehall–Westminster model prescribes that the Cabinet holds collective responsibility, which implies that ministers are bound by the decisions of the Cabinet, even when they had no part in their discussion or decision.

There must be at least thirteen other ministers, each of whom have a portfolio or specific ministry, or are designated 'Minister without Portfolio'. Cabinet members must be members of one of the two Houses of Parliament, either the Senate (no more than four) or the elected House of Representatives. In Cabinet meetings, ministers present bills (proposed laws) related to their ministerial portfolio as a first step to enacting new legislation. Cabinet examines these bills, especially the costs, and recommends to ministers whether bills should proceed to Parliament or changes should be made.

Cabinet appointments are made at the discretion of the prime minister, though he or she may consult with others to decide on the appointments. After any election, party members and supporters, especially those who won their seats and those who played key roles in the victory, wait to get a call from the new prime minister. The wait can be excruciating, especially if you know that others have already gotten calls. You question where you are in the pecking order, or if you are going to get a call at all. But a prime minister can only call one person at a time.

After the 2007 election, I was not expecting to be among the first phone calls from Prime Minister Golding. So when he called me in his office and told me he wanted me to go to Agriculture as a full Minister I was initially surprised. I did not expect to be appointed to the Cabinet. I would never have assumed that as I had never known of a first-term MP being elevated to the office of a full minister. Moreover, the closest I had been to agriculture was my backyard garden with a few roots of cane. But it was important to accept what I was given, and I did so immediately. Aside from my shock at the appointment, the portfolio intimidated me. He said to me, 'You have a discipline and skill in management and what this portfolio needs is management. Make agriculture relevant again.' In that regard, I was certainly qualified for that and probably any other Cabinet position, but political appointments in Jamaica do not have a history of being based on merit.

Not having been in any other cabinet I don't have a basis of comparison, but Jamaica's Cabinet is well managed, modern, organized, and efficient. Even in the absence of all the desired resources, the Cabinet secretary and his/her team work hard to ensure that there is no lapse in logistics or coordination, and that Cabinet meetings run smoothly.

Cabinet meetings are a world unto themselves. They usually last all day; it makes no sense to plan anything else that day. The issues of poor health and weight gain that plague many Cabinet members can in part be attributed to that one day each week where you get little physical activity and where you have no choice in what you are fed.

Week in, week out, you are locked in a room with the same people, some that you agree with, some that you don't, some who your spirit takes to, and some who rub you the wrong way. You learn a lot about your Cabinet colleagues because you spend so much time around them. I can't think of any other experience since living on hall at university where I have so regularly interacted with the same group of people over such a long period of time. You come to appreciate the colourful dynamics of the different personalities at work. There is a lot of laughter, confusion, seriousness, and sometimes anger. You have to learn how to negotiate, explain things in ways that make sense to everyone else, how to carry your argument, and how to convince your colleagues.

The general path of a policy is that a minister pilots a submission linked to his or her portfolio that describes a situation and calls for a course of action whether via policy or legislation. Relevant technocrats may attend the meeting for that part of the discussion to support that presentation. Then everyone weighs in and debates the issue. Dialogue and discussion ensue, often heated, sometimes frustrating, sometimes rewarding. The resulting decision is a collective one; it doesn't matter who brought it to Cabinet, it is signed off by the group and the group owns it.

The main method of approval of Cabinet decisions is consensus. Arriving at consensus usually entails long and detailed discussions, and often disagreements, of all aspects of whatever policy is being proposed. It means that regardless of one's specific ministry or portfolio, Cabinet members all know what each other is doing, and learn many of the intricacies of the other ministries and their work. We are all in there to discuss the nation's business and to take decisions, knowing that often times even after extensive, hours-long discussion and a painfully hammered out consensus, the decision will then get delayed or even thwarted by the bureaucracy. It is a training ground in how government works like no other.

One such decision was about drafting a new Fisheries Act. During my tenure as Minister of Agriculture and Fisheries, I revived the process of updating the 1976 Fisheries Act. Review of the law had started in 1995 under the People's National Party (PNP). I commissioned a management audit of the ministry shortly after I assumed my position there, in 2008, and the audit made clear that this was a key area of concern. The need was dire: we had no legislation against poaching or unregulated fishing, no modern and relevant licensing regulations, and the existing laws prevented us from creating a more enabling environment for sustainable growth in the sector. The Cabinet decision then was to approve drafting instructions. Towards the end of 2018, 24 years after the process started, the bill was finally passed.

After my very first Cabinet meeting, I recognized the awesome responsibility that the position carried and the inherent conflicts in trying to get the work done. Together with just over a dozen other people, we carried the responsibility of moving the country forward. But at the same time each Cabinet member is a member of a political organization that requires popular support for them to stay in their job. One of the greatest challenges is to distinguish and delink those roles as one is so much influenced by the other. Where does national interest conflict with political interest? We faced this question many times especially with the issues related to agriculture. With citrus, with sugar, with bananas, crops that are labour intensive means that votes are involved. In addition, we have so much sentiment attached to agriculture that it is difficult for rationality to prevail. A lot of those decisions emanated from me given my portfolio. I tended towards rationality over sentiment, and so I had to do the work to bring some of my colleagues to agree to a realistic position when politically they felt it could be dangerous. There was a similar dynamic with the divestment of Air Jamaica. The sentiment attached to having our own national airline, such a symbol of Jamaican pride for decades, made it political dynamite. But the airline was haemorrhaging billions of dollars, had never been profitable despite many efforts, and likely never would be. It is an ongoing tension that will exist as long as we continue in the Westminster system.

One of the National Democratic Movement's (NDM's) original proposals was for a separation of powers that would have made the executive non-elected, as it is in the US, so that decisions would be taken that would not have to take popular support into consideration. The counter argument is that Cabinet members should have a connection to the people on the ground. It is for that reason that the Minister of Finance has to be an elected MP. For effective and realistic policy to be made, the thinking goes, Cabinet members must have a connection to the ordinary people who will be affected by their decisions.

There is also an ongoing tension between those who are appointed to the executive and those elected representatives who remain without a government appointment, the so-called backbenchers. The Cabinet has a responsibility to represent them and their constituents' interests just as much as they do their own. Further, many decisions have to go through a parliamentary process, where they need the support of the government MPs, particularly when the majority is very slim, as it was with the Jamaica Labour Party (JLP) in 2007–2011.

Running a government – running a country – is an inherently unpredictable task. Crises, natural disasters and unexpected and unintended developments pop up every day that have to be dealt with, some immediately, in one's own portfolio, and in the nation's business. The balance between responsibility to the nation, the political interests of one's own constituency, and the needs of parliamentary colleagues is an ongoing but requisite challenge. My time in my own portfolio ministry, Agriculture and Fisheries, brought that home to me at every turn.

23

Cassava Man

When I was appointed Minister of Agriculture and Fisheries it came as a surprise to me. I was not in a position to question Bruce Golding on the appointment, and I was grateful and honoured to be appointed to the Cabinet, so I accepted and set to work.

Within his or her ministry, each minister's role is to carry though the government's policy via programmes and projects, whose execution is the responsibility of the technocrats – the non-political civil servants – in the ministry, led by the Permanent Secretary. Those policies ought to be extensions of the party's general platform that took it into office, and what the party represents.

Once the minister assumes office they would also review policies that are in train and carry them forward, if they are in agreement. It is the Permanent Secretary and the Ministry public servant staff who are tasked with implementing the programmes that fulfil the policies as determined by the minister. This is the theory. The reality is that a new minister with a lot of energy and ideas, and an intention to create some sort of legacy, can have his or her policy ideas seriously stymied by a ministry staff that either does not have the capacity, or the will, to see them through. Or, in interpreting the minister's policy their understanding is different from the minister's intention. Yet it is the minister and not the civil servant who is held responsible to Parliament and the public for the success or failure of policies or programmes.

In practice a minister, particularly an 'activist minister' – someone who is immersed in the job, keen to move policy forward, and determined for changes to happen – does more than that. That minister has to advocate for his or her policies – within Cabinet so the policy is approved and adopted by the government, within the public sphere to get buy-in and support, and sometimes even within the ministry so that the technocrats he or she relies on are motivated do their part in bringing the policy to life. Where things can get dicey is when a minister tries to drive the implementation process; maintaining the appropriate boundaries can be frustrating when there is work to be done and nothing seems to be moving forward. It is one of the greatest challenges I have faced during my time as a government minister.

I was determined to make my mark in whatever ministry I was assigned to, and I was going to do whatever it took to make a positive difference. If it was to be agriculture, so be it.

The Ministry of Agriculture and Fisheries is not considered a 'plum' ministry, and none of the senior Jamaica Labour Party (JLP) people would have wanted it, but I would like to think that Golding recognized its importance and scope, and saw me as a strong leader who could take that ministry's mandate to a new level. Nearly 18 per cent of the country's labour force, some 200,000 farmers and their families, depend on agriculture for their primary source of income. The multiplier impact is significant.

Agriculture contributes approximately six per cent of GDP. This clearly indicates an economic activity that affects thousands, but many of those thousands are living on the margins of society. Six per cent of GDP to share for 18 per cent of the labour force is a small pie sharing for many mouths.

On the face of it this was an attractive ministry to work in, with a broad scope to have a positive impact on the country's situation and on many people's lives, but it was also an incredibly difficult portfolio to work with, if one wanted to see real improvement and positive results.

Once I was in the ministry, despite a lack of direct experience working in agriculture, farming, or fisheries, I quickly realized that I could bring my existing training and experience to the position. This was a position that I would have qualified for if the process was one of appointing persons as one would in a normal job application process. My academic training and research, as well as my experience with the farmers and fisherfolk in my constituency, prepared me well for the tasks ahead.

My entrepreneurial traits and experiences would also prove useful. I had experienced business at many different levels. Besides my consulting and the barbershop in May Pen, my time as an informal commercial exporter while I was at UWI grounded me in the nitty-gritty of value chains, doing business with small producers, and the nature of exports for niche products – all critical elements of Jamaican agriculture.

I also had studied the demand for Jamaican goods for my master's thesis at Georgia State. At the time when I did my master's, and 12 years later when I was appointed minister, a key question was: Why is it that we were known then – and before that and up to now – as 'a nation of samples'?

There are outliers, like the world famous Pickapeppa Sauce which has been produced in Manchester for nearly a hundred years and can be found in supermarkets all over the world. But in large part, we have not maximized our potential in agriculture or in the manufacturing of products like Pickapeppa Sauce that are made with our excellent Jamaican agricultural products.

I had always known that agriculture and farming are essential to Jamaica at many different levels, but I didn't fully understand why we had not fulfilled our potential in farming. Why are we so challenged to efficiently produce, market, and export our agricultural products? What is it that prevents us from growing and selling more of our world-famous Blue Mountain Coffee, ginger, or cocoa? Or from making world-class value-added products with them, which we can sell at higher margins, rather than exporting the unfinished products to others who then refine them and add value to them?

These questions had long ago sparked my recognition that policy was important to promoting the necessary changes, and I was already convinced that government policy was a tool for national development in this regard. I set about figuring out what were the necessary policy responses to these questions, and the Ministry of Agriculture and Fisheries was the ideal place to do this.

The solution lies in improving the productivity and competitiveness of farmers and farming practices, and this can only be done by modernizing agriculture and establishing a value chain approach where there is greater dialogue on supply and pricing between producer and processor (or producer and distributor). Suppliers and processors/distributors work together to plan and organize, to identify and remedy weak spots in the supply chain, to ensure that farmers are adequately financed, and to coordinate small farmers to operate cohesively. As straightforward as the solution appeared, however, this would require a change of mindset and a profound systemic change at all levels of the agricultural system as it is now practised in Jamaica – a task beyond any single minister to easily undertake in a four-year term, which in the reality of Jamaica's political cycle is really only two and a half years in which one can actually get things done.

One of the first things I did was add 'and Fisheries' to the ministry's name, as fisherfolk and the fishing industry fall under the ministry's mandate, but weren't reflected in the name of the ministry. It was more than a cosmetic change. I wanted this neglected population, which I knew well as there were many fisherfolk in my own constituency, to feel included and represented. I intended for the ministry to place a great deal more emphasis on fisheries in its work.

One of the aspects of my job as minister that I had to educate myself on and come to properly understand was to know who the Jamaican farmer is, and what his or her needs are. He or she represents 18 per cent of Jamaica's workforce, a significant proportion. He or she, typically, is around 55 years old, with no formal training in agriculture or otherwise, and occupying and working a small parcel of land – two to five acres – for which he or she has no registered title.

The Jamaican farmer has little or no access to credit, would have little to no understanding of the vagaries and idiosyncrasies of the international trading system that affect him or her directly, and would be unlikely to access or benefit from re-tooling or re-training.

This is the understanding that I brought to looking at Jamaican agriculture in the global context. While one might argue that we do our farmers and especially young people born in farming and rural areas a disservice if we allow them to continue in an industry or occupation for which there is no future, we also have to recognize that we all have an obligation to the existing farmer as a human being, and as a significant bloc of Jamaican citizens, to recognize their contribution and to do what we can to ensure that they are able to live fulfilling and worthwhile lives.

The second task was to understand all the different ways that farming and agriculture were important for Jamaica, aside from the livelihood and well-being of a sizable proportion of the population, particularly in the rural parts of the island. The two main aspects of agriculture's importance are the domestic food supply, and production of primary and value-added foodstuffs for export.

Ensuring that agriculture is able to meet the domestic demand for food is not a simple equation in Jamaica. I talked a lot about food security at the beginning of my tenure as Agriculture Minister. Food security is one of those topics that can be argued about until the end of time. The economists will say that the notion of food security is outdated and that in a global market, such as the one we live in now, the consumer pays the price for protecting domestic producers when there are cheaper sources, via imports, of equivalent foodstuffs.

But there are also many arguments that favour government policies that proactively support agriculture with a view to food security. Even though I have a doctorate in business, which included studying economics, my first approach to a policy question or policy issue is what makes sense to me intuitively. Then I will harness the data and the research, and listen to the various arguments, and figure out for myself my position.

It did not make sense to me, despite the economists' arguments, that we would import a food item from another country that we can produce here, when the imported item is cheaper only because that country's government is subsidizing that producer. As long as countries provide direct and/or indirect subsidies to their own producers and farmers, there will never be a truly free global market, and it is only to our detriment that we create policies and take actions that are in line with a so-called global free market that does not truly exist, while other producers are not playing by those rules.

There are other considerations besides economics and aspects of food importation that go beyond numbers. Especially when it concerns agricultural imports, fresh food is always better and healthier. The shortest time between farm to table is optimal for foods to retain their nutritional value. Imported fresh foods by definition have spent a great deal of time in transit and would not have equivalent nutritional value to local products, even if the local products are a bit more expensive, which is not always the case.

Apart from guaranteeing a consistent supply of food for our citizens, I came to see agriculture and fisheries as important aspects of Jamaica's development prospects. After just a few months on the job, I came to the conclusion that farming, fishing, and agriculture were the solutions for many of Jamaica's problems, including and primarily the issues of rural poverty and underdevelopment. These are not groundbreaking or original insights, but being in the middle of it brought it home to me.

Much of my work at the Ministry of Agriculture and Fisheries was concerned with how to resolve immediate challenges with longer term views on how to make Jamaican agriculture and fishing a more viable and productive industry overall. I took decisions that though not popular, were necessary for the country's development, and the shift from a declining agricultural sector to one that would create the wealth Jamaica so desperately needs.

I also learned firsthand the tradeoffs between policies that are intended to promote national interests and their effects on the ground, particularly as they translate to political support. In fisheries we embarked on an ambitious programme to establish fish sanctuaries around the island, in an attempt to reverse our serious problem of overfishing. We also changed the rules regarding the size of nets, to protect smaller and younger fish.

When we launched this initiative Jamaica was one of the most overfished areas in the Western Atlantic. The programme had some successes, and fish stocks started to rebound in almost all the areas where sanctuaries were established. But local fishermen, including many in my own constituency, were not happy with the new rules. For them, the sustainability of the fishing industry was a distant concept when it meant that their catch that day was down. I am quite sure that I lost quite a few fisherfolk votes in my constituency in the 2011 election, as a result of those new rules.

It brought home to me why it is often so difficult for politicians, once in office, to implement difficult decisions that are necessary for medium and long-term progress and change, particularly at the national level, when small local groups would consider themselves disenfranchised as a result. Again, the clash of political interest versus national interest comes to the fore. It speaks to our political maturity, the way we communicate policies and policy changes, particularly to the people who they will affect the most, and to the provisions for those groups that are the losers in such situations.

On the food production side, we emphasized many key areas geared at improving competitiveness and efficiencies in the sector. These included greenhouse farming, hot pepper nurseries, ginger and potato rehabilitation programmes, small irrigation systems, agro-park clusters for value-added production, backyard and school garden programmes, and farmers' markets.

The initiative which garnered the most media attention was in cassava. I announced the programme to increase cassava production in my first budget speech. The PNP used this to accuse me of trying to return Jamaicans to the days of slavery.

I was then branded 'Cassava Man'. It did not bother me at the time, but I did feel a quiet sense of vindication when the administration changed and the new PNP agriculture minister, Roger Clarke, embraced cassava as a useful local product for a range of uses. When I initiated a rice-cultivation project in 2009 Roger Clarke made fun of the effort saying that it would take more than five acres to prove rice was viable because he alone could consume that five acres. Yet, just four months after taking office as Minister of Agriculture, Clarke announced a J$120 million rice project. Good policies are good policies, whichever party puts them forward. In all three ministries I have been in charge of I have continued with those policies that are promising, regardless of who conceptualized them. We criticize the actions and policies of the opposing party just for criticism's sake, rather than really examining the merits or lack thereof and giving credit or laying blame where it is really due.

I was gratified by the public support I received and was heartened by the recognition of my efforts in the Ministry of Agriculture and Fisheries. During 2009, the agricultural sector recorded some 13 per cent growth and there was a decline of 75 per cent in fresh food imports, largely due to the initiatives we had started. I am proud of the work we did, and it was indeed a team effort.

The internal support I had in the ministry was especially meaningful for me personally. When I first walked through the doors at Old Hope Road in September 2007 the resentment and negativity in the air were palpable. Once it became clear what I was about – that I genuinely aimed to change things for the better, and I would stop at nothing for that to happen – the staff morale lifted tremendously.

Within a few months the temperature at the ministry was upbeat, positive, and everyone there was raring to go. But along with the highs, there were also many lows.

24

BITTER SUGAR

I was honoured in 2010 when the influential *Gleaner* newspaper named me its Man of the Year, and cited my work and achievements in the Ministry of Agriculture and Fisheries. I accepted the award with humility and credited the team at the ministry for this achievement.

My motivation to succeed in my position was about more than augmenting my national profile. I sincerely believed in the potential of agriculture and fisheries to not only improve the prospects of its stakeholders but also for the overall development of Jamaica's economy and people. But I was criticized for some of the actions I took. This is par for the course for any leader; I have always known and accepted that.

It is inevitable that in Jamaica, as in most other countries, whichever party is in opposition will seek to capitalize on whatever opportunity they can, to undermine the government for their own political gain. But in Jamaica too often we take it too far, even to the point of being illogical and unreasonable. I am always amazed – naively, perhaps – that political leaders are ready to criticize a programme in opposition they endorsed while in government. It's a part of the tribal nature of the politics and can be quite frustrating because it forestalls meaningful debate and consensus around critical common goals.

The default orientation that the opposition must always oppose everything the government does is immature and injurious to the country's democratic development. It was Edward Seaga who put it most succinctly when he said in 2003 that the role of the opposition is to 'oppose, oppose, oppose'. I believe in an opposition that is strident and critical where it must speak out on all relevant issues and policies, but not to oppose for opposing's sake.

I do not think the role of any opposition is just to criticize, or, as some politicians have said in the past, keep its ideas secret for fear that the opponent take it and try to own it. Our democracy is predicated on competing ideas and political parties must be nimble and versatile enough to compete for attention and acceptance of the electorate around the ideas it puts forward.

Unfortunately the notion of consensus between government and opposition is anathema to the Jamaican polity, and it prevents a great deal of work from being done. It also creates uncertainty, which leads to a poor investment climate, when opposition parties make threats about discontinuing policies and projects 'once they return to office'.

Divestment is one of those areas that the opposition constantly politicizes, as it is an easy target to rile up nationalist sentiment with simplistic rhetoric. It is an area that is not understood by many Jamaicans, and opposition politicians take advantage of this ignorance for their own short-sighted purposes. In Jamaica, we have a knee-jerk bias against divestment and privatization that has been engendered by many of our intellectual elite and transmitted through the tertiary and even the secondary education system.

I came under heavy fire for the divestments that I set about completing when I was Minister of Agriculture and Fisheries, even the ones that had been started by the People's National Party (PNP) administration before I came into office. This is one of the areas of political communication where the Jamaica

Labour Party (JLP) was weak then, and where I didn't take up the task myself because I didn't appreciate its importance. The public relations and marketing work to communicate and put a positive spin on policies and initiatives is essential in modern-day politics. I didn't realize then the imperative to put in the extra effort to portray everything you do in a positive light. Policies seldom speak for themselves. (Bear in mind that this was 2008–2010 – prior to the advent of political marketing on social media which emerged in Jamaica a few years later, in 2015–16, and which, as I write this in 2019, is ubiquitous.)

One of the policy goals of the new JLP administration from the outset was to divest entities owned by the state that were not profitable and ought rightfully be better placed in the private sector. These divestments were done to mitigate the losses – many of these state-owned entities had become huge liabilities, and were sucking up vast portions of government spending – as one of the necessary steps towards debt restructuring, as well as to give these entities a fair chance to justify their existence in a changing world economy.

More fundamental was the issue of the role of government in a changing world dispensation. Should government operate and be responsible for non-essential services, like airlines and sugar estates? Or should they focus on critical functions like security and justice, hospitals, and schools?

This is a relevant debate in today's Jamaica, especially as a country that is so heavily indebted and where our tax revenues are unable to adequately provide basic services. Even in the case of some essential services, the time has come for the Jamaican government to consider divesting itself, at least partially, of some of them. Whether through public–private partnerships or wholesale privatizations, there is a dire need to attract critical capital injection to replace dilapidated infrastructure. Water, sewage systems, roads, and prisons are just a few areas that could benefit from these types of partnerships. Careful thought is needed to develop the terms of reference in order to protect the public interest while motivating the private investor. Jamaica badly needs expertise in this area.

The JLP administration of 2007–2011 made an important start as we took the first steps to rid ourselves of some of the most obvious debt-riddled entities. In most cases, the entities that were divested were not earning any net profit. Indeed, they were costing taxpayers dearly to keep the doors open and the plants running. Though it wasn't my portfolio, the divestment of Air Jamaica was a prime case in point. The airline, from its inception, had cost the Jamaican people, despite benefiting only a small percentage of the population, even given the so-called multiplier effect that it was claimed the airline had on tourism. In just the last three years before it was sold, Jamaican taxpayers spent some J$40 billion keeping the airline going.

While it was emotionally difficult to let go of Air Jamaica, we simply could not afford to keep it, and we paid a steep price maintaining it for as long as we did. But there was a mindset among many Jamaican people that Air Jamaica was a symbol of national pride, and to do away with it was somehow disloyal.

There were similar paradoxical sentiments about some of the divestments that I was engaged in as minister, sugar chief among them. The sugar industry in independent Jamaica has been for the most part unprofitable and unsustainable. Free and forced labour was essential to sugar being profitable, and without that free labour and significant preferential treatments that equated to subsidies for African, Caribbean and Pacific (ACP) countries, Jamaica and other Caribbean countries lost their advantage as sugar producers in the world market.

Lack of profitability led to unmaintained factories and fields and further deterioration in productivity. In the mid 1960s, Jamaica produced over 500,000 tonnes of sugar per year. In over three years of government control of five estates total production in the country never passed 150,000 tonnes of sugar. And this was before the introduction of other much more competitive sugar producers into the market.

Over the decades, the industry has become more mechanized with the introduction of increasingly sophisticated technology. Jamaica fell further and further behind other large sugar producers, such as Brazil and India. Our cost of production is higher than most other countries in the world.

For many decades we did not have to compete, so it did not matter if our sugar was more expensive. As a colony under British rule we had a guaranteed market in England and the price was not an issue. After independence we had arrangements with European countries for them to continue buying our sugar at a certain price, whether or not there was sugar available from other countries that was cheaper.

What evolved from all these different pricing regimes was a complicated system where we sold our sugar for a high price, bought sugar from overseas producers for local consumption at a lower price, and used the difference to keep the sugar industry going. We had a complicated and distorted market, inefficient production, and an industry that employed thousands of unskilled people who would have had no other possibility of getting a job outside of sugar.

As time went on, we got more inefficient at producing sugar, and taxpayers' money was keeping the sugar industry afloat. Between 2001 and 2007 alone, Jamaican taxpayers paid over J$20 billion to keep the sugar industry alive.

The JLP administration that took office in September 2007 inherited the attempt to sell state-owned sugar assets, an initiative that had started under the PNP in 2005. If there is one area where there is no partisan political disagreement it is over resolving the sugar problem. Yet the opposition did not miss an opportunity to be critical of the process once we took it on. They politicized it and portrayed it as a 'selling out' of the country's patrimony.

As soon as I assumed office I appointed a new team to resume the privatization process of the five sugar estates owned by the state. We had to act quickly because the agreement we had with the Europeans for so many years was going to end in September 2009, and we would have had no buyer for our expensive sugar, and no way of paying workers to reap the crop without a buyer.

We went through an extensive process of soliciting bids and examining the offers. The level of scrutiny that is now applied to the sale of government assets is rigorous. In the past ten years, strict rules have been introduced that accompany any sale of government property, and there is usually a committee of people from the private and public sector, all representing different interests, who oversee and manage the process. The Contractor General closely monitors every step. It would be difficult and unusual in Jamaica today for there to be a dishonest transaction involving the sale of a state-owned asset.

Even though there were initially some verbal expressions of interest by local entities for the state-owned assets, there were no formal proposals from any Jamaican investor to purchase anything once the official tender was launched. There were some local players who were desirous of obtaining parts of some estates, but their proposals amounted to stripping the assets of their more valuable parts, rendering the remaining components redundant.

I refused to allow this to happen and that was yet another source of heavy criticism. I was warned that if I didn't portion out the assets they would never sell. I was even reported to the Prime Minister for naivety and not knowing what I was doing. Fortunately Golding did not come in my way and I continued on my course, but I suspected that I was not winning any popularity contests among the existing sugar interests at the time.

Having complied with the procurement process, and with no local takers, an acceptable offer was made by a Brazilian company, Infinity Bio-Energy. It met all the terms of the tender and the divestment team approved it. Announcements were made and we thought it was a done deal.

But Infinity failed to secure the financing and the deal collapsed at the last minute. That was extremely disappointing, and somewhat embarrassing, because we had been through so much to get to the point of selling these five sugar estates, with a great deal of media attention, public scrutiny and misunderstanding about the process.

We went back to advertising the properties and started all over again. The next promising expression of interest was an Italian company, Eridania Suisse, which indicated an interest in purchasing all five government estates. We went through a complicated and intense negotiation with Eridania, and a US$15 million advance payment was agreed on which allowed the next crop to be saved. So precarious was the industry that we had to scramble for bridge financing at short notice, from a prospective buyer, no less. The Italians would eventually tell us that they were not interested in purchasing so we parted company after we delivered on our commitments.

The process of divesting started yet again. We repackaged the assets and on that go-round we were able to attract a number of expressions of interest, including from a Chinese entity and two local companies.

At last things were progressing and negotiations began in earnest. It was a massive task involving many organizations. All the critical stakeholders participated, including cane farmers, trade unions, potential purchasers, the regulator, and the government. The lawyers were engaged to make the multiple transactions, including land transfers and consolidation and final contracts legally possible.

The Development Bank of Jamaica, the divestment team, Ministry of Agriculture and Fisheries personnel, the European Union in Jamaica, and the Prime Minister and Cabinet were all involved. The divestment of the sugar estates was by far the most complex and challenging task that I undertook as a minister of government and the one that, at the time, I was most proud of.

By August 2011, the Chinese company that had built the cricket stadium in Trelawny and the Convention Centre in Montego Bay – Complant, later trading as Pan Caribbean Sugar – bought Monymusk, Frome, and Bernard Lodge. Duckenfield in St Thomas and Long Pond in Trelawny were purchased by Jamaican investors.

In addition to the sale of the government estates, I presided over a sugar transformation process that saw the proposition of a new restructured regulatory framework. A commission of inquiry chaired by UWI Professor Alvin Wint recommended a major programme of retraining and resettlement for over 3,000 workers who were displaced prior to divestment. These workers received a combination of retraining, cash, and land to pursue alternative economic endeavours.

The process was not perfect but was sufficient to ensure a successful transition and the cooperation of the trade union leaders.

Other Caribbean countries have completely shuttered their sugar industries, for various reasons. Trinidad and Tobago closed its sugar factories in 2003 because they did not want to continue putting the cost of the industry onto taxpayers. In their estimation, it was more cost-effective to pay out the 8,000 sugar workers than to keep the industry going. Patrick Manning vowed that as long as he was prime minister sugar workers would never go back to cutting cane, that it would be like going back to slavery.

Antigua and Barbuda ended its sugar industry because, they said, they wanted to rid themselves of any vestiges of slavery. Cuba, once the producer of 25 per cent of the world's sugar, dramatically downsized its industry in the aftermath of the collapse of the Soviet Union and the corresponding loss of their guaranteed market and subsidized oil supply. Without the economic space to modernize, nor to subsidize the industry themselves, as we have done in Jamaica, and as Trinidad and Tobago did for so many decades, they reduced production to meet domestic demand.

In Jamaica, we are faced with all of these issues, so why did we choose then to keep the industry alive?

In Jamaica, despite the noises and complaints from the PNP during the divestment, there is rare political consensus on the realities of totally abandoning cane cultivation: neither side is willing to do it. There are too many jobs at stake, and too many people's lives would be affected. We had to reorganize the industry so it would have a better chance of being profitable, and new investment was required for that.

The most important lesson I took from the entire experience of the sugar divestment is that as a country we have to rethink the place of sugar in our history and our society. We can't change the past. We can't change our history. We have many books written by historians and other great thinkers about the role of sugar in slavery, in colonialism, and in the poor working and living conditions of sugar cane cutters. There is no shortage of knowledge on the negatives of sugar. But we have to come to a point where we move on. Dwelling on the past and on the negatives gets us nowhere and achieves nothing. We have had enough time to come to terms with it, and we have decided we are staying with sugar.

I saw firsthand the need for a mindset change in the sugar industry as a first step to move the industry forward. We had to cease seeing cane cultivation and sugar production as a symbol of slavery, but rather as an economic opportunity to be modernized and made efficient and competitive. Not an easy task because the mindset of the stakeholders is still very much in that mode. In the divestment negotiations, I was shocked at how entrenched outmoded attitudes and patterns of thinking were. The factory and landowners and the sugar cane workers continue to feel entitled to whatever it is they have always felt is owed them – even when those entitlements are, today, outdated and regressive.

Today, the dream of a new and improved sugar industry has been dashed by the reality of fluctuating but generally lower world prices, lingering low productivity issues, failed attempts at value-added integration, and fast-fading interest by once enthusiastic investors. As I write this in 2019, to my and I am sure many others' great disappointment, the government is being called on for yet another bailout. It is clear that our latest attempts at divesting for sustainability have not worked. It should also be clear that we cannot go back whence we came. My own personal view is shifting: cane sugar and its by-products are simply not viable or practicable for Jamaica, and I am not hopeful that there is an attainable economic model for us, given how many efforts have been made over so many years. It appears decision-time on the future of sugar is here, and whether it is a JLP or a PNP government, one of us is going to have to make some tough decisions.

At the time of this writing, in 2019, there has been ongoing tumult in the sector, from Complant suspending production, Golden Grove on the brink of closing, and the government is back in the middle, intervening at virtually every level, from canecutter to supermarket shelf.

How is it that we could find ourselves right back in this position, after all that transpired? Was it that the companies didn't make the investments that they had planned to, or was it that the unpredictable nature of markets and business didn't favour them, and their projected earnings and profits didn't materialize? The diversification into ethanol and other sugar by-products appears not to have occurred – most likely because the prices are too low to justify the investment necessary. But these are now private companies in whose interest it would have been to diversify for their own future viability. There are no easy answers for the sugar industry, and once again, difficult choices are in front of the government, and the stakeholders in the sugar industry, as they have the jobs and livelihoods of many tens of thousands of people in jeopardy.

In every aspect of our lives, as individuals, and as a country, we come to crossroads where we have to make decisions, or sometimes the decision is made for us and we are left with the choice of how to react and cope. In my personal life, I had to face just such a challenge, with the unexpected death of my mother.

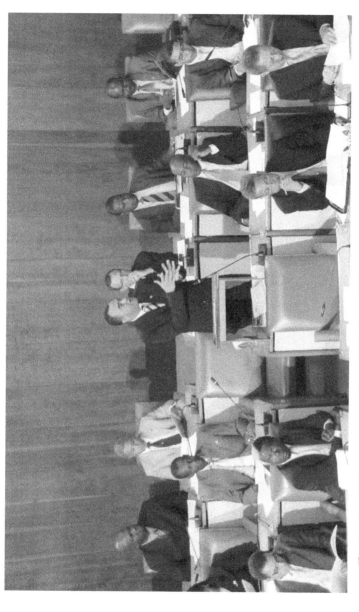

First sectoral debate presentation as Minister of Agriculture and Fisheries, April 15, 2008.
Courtesy of the Jamaica Information Service.

Touring the Amity Hall Rice Project as Minister of Agriculture and Fisheries with L-R: Christopher Levy of Jamaica Broilers, Roger Clarke Opposition (PNP) spokesman on agriculture, and Richard Sadler, July 6, 2009. Though we were political opponents I had a great deal of respect and fondness for Roger Clarke.
Courtesy of the Gleaner Company (Media) Ltd.

With Prime Minister Bruce Golding (far left) and Horace Chang, Minister of Water, Environment and Housing, at official opening of pump house at Hopewell, St. Elizabeth. October 23, 2010.
Photo courtesy Jamaica Information Service.

With all my siblings as we gathered for our mother's funeral in 2010.
Sharon Miller, Andrew Blake, Shelly-Ann Blake and Brian Sutherland.

Photo: personal collection CT.

Family portrait – Charles, Neadene, Kimberly and Adam, 2012.
Photo: personal collection CT.

I was co-executive director of a public policy think tank while out of office 2012–2016. Dr Damien King, was the other co-executive director at the Caribbean Policy Research Institute (CAPRI), 2015.

Courtesy of CAPRI.

Nomination Day in West Central St Catherine, February 9, 2016.
Photo: personal collection CT.

With Prime Minister Andrew Holness (then Leader of the Opposition for the JLP) campaigning in West Central St Catherine, February 14, 2016.
Photo: personal collection CT.

*With my fellow members of parliament walking to Gordon House
for the ceremonial opening of Parliament, April 14, 2016.*
Courtesy of the Jamaica Information Service.

*Running the Good Samaritan 5K Run-Walk
with Senator Floyd Morris, August 26, 2018.*
Courtesy of Market Me Consulting Limited.

With children of Seaward Primary and Junior High School, Phase 3 of Obesity Prevention Campaign Launch, October 12, 2018.
Courtesy of the Ministry of Health.

Official reopening of the Hagley Park Health Centre. L–R: Everton W. Anderson, Maureen Golding and former Prime Minister, the Most Hon. Portia Simpson Miller. July 4, 2017.
Courtesy of the National Health Fund.

25

Ruby

Midway through my time at the Ministry of Agriculture, in 2009, my mother died. She was only 64, and I felt cheated. She was young and had so much life left in her. I wanted more time with her, and I wanted my children to have more time with her, to know her better, to feel her love. She was being treated for breast cancer and a confluence of factors contributed to her having a fatal stroke. It was unexpected and I was devastated.

My mother provided me with the foundation of who I am today – her character, her dedication to her goals, her work ethic. She was not exposed to higher levels of learning until she was an adult, but she was blessed with a sharp intellect and wit. Her training was in shorthand and typing – clerical skills, not untypical for someone from her socio-economic background. If you had a conversation with her, you would never know she came from such modest beginnings. She spoke perfect English and had a good grasp of the issues of the day.

As a mature person my mother subscribed to traditional values. She was careful about what we were exposed to, and did her best to instil conservative values in us. Our education was her first priority, yet at one point she turned down a scholarship offer that one of my siblings received because it came from a company in the gaming business and she was against gambling.

She joined the church when she moved back to Mandeville: Battersea United Brethren. She was a devout fundamentalist Christian. She spent a lot of time at church throughout the week and was extremely active as a choir member. She was a great singer and sang at every opportunity and occasion she got. She later trained for and was ordained a minister in her church.

My mother was ambitious in her goals for herself and for her children. She wanted to own her own home, which she did. She wanted to be financially independent, which she was. Work was important to her, not only for the earnings, but she truly believed in the value of hard work and of contributing to society through work and service.

She took her job as a labour officer seriously. She worked with the farm workers' programme in the Ministry of Labour and Social Security. When the lists came down with the names of the people who should report to the Mandeville Horticultural Showground, with short notice, she would personally go and find each of them, in whatever district they resided. When the farm workers returned from their stints abroad, many would bring her gifts as an indication of their gratitude.

My mother was kind and compassionate, always aware that there were people less fortunate than herself, and always doing what she could to help them. The lifelong lesson I learnt from my mother is that hard work eventually pays off, stay the course for what you believe in, and give back to society as best as you can as there is always someone less fortunate. My mother was especially good at managing a crisis. She was articulate and analytical, and she always remained calm, something I would also like to think that she passed on to me. Gone too soon, I felt…a feeling that grew stronger very soon after she passed as I wished she was there in some of the turbulent times about to come.

For us, her five children, she ensured that we developed a sense of responsibility by giving us chores around the house, and being a strict disciplinarian. Even when we bucked heads when I was a teenager, as I didn't always agree with how strict she was, her guidance and her expectations of me continued to guide me. Knowing that she was proud of me when I did well helped me to always strive to make her even prouder.

My siblings and I have all enjoyed success in pursuing our academic goals and career choices. My sister Sharon is a senior career diplomat in the Ministry of Foreign Affairs and Foreign Trade, and has served Jamaica diligently for decades. My brother Brian, as mentioned earlier, joined the Jamaica Constabulary Force after he completed his first degree at UWI, did a postgraduate degree in England in security administration at the prestigious Cranfield University, and later migrated to Canada where he took a position in the Toronto Police Force. Shelly trained for and became an intensive care nurse at the University Hospital of the West Indies and later moved to St Ann where she resides with her preacher husband and now teaches nursing. My mother's last child, Andrew, studied at the Seminary and is Dean of Discipline at a high school in rural Jamaica.

When I entered representational politics, it was entirely with my mother's blessing. She followed my political career closely and openly prayed for me, engaged with me, encouraged me, and supported me, especially when I was being publicly criticized.

Even though I was bitter that she was taken so soon, I will always be comforted in the fact that she lived a good life and that she contributed a great deal to her community and her country, and that all her children have been successful in their own lives. But as much as I try to rationalize this with myself, I still miss her badly.

26

DEPUTY LEADER

In addition to my ministerial duties, and my responsibility as Member of Parliament, I had a senior position in the Jamaica Labour Party (JLP) and a duty to continue my work building the party. In late 2010, I took on a new leadership position within the JLP when I ran for and won the position of deputy leader for Area Council Four, which covers western Jamaica. I defeated Horace Chang, a JLP stalwart, in a bitter race. But it didn't start out that way.

I've heard it said that my running for deputy leader when I did was premature and that I was pushing the limits and bucking the traditional way of moving up in the party hierarchy. There is some truth to this: relative to most others' paths in the JLP – and in the People's National Party (PNP) – I had moved quickly. I re-joined the party having left as an insignificant Young Jamaica member, and after having taken a leadership role in a break-away, rival party. I became general secretary, then president of Generation 2000 (G2K), was appointed a senator, convincingly won my parliamentary seat, and was appointed a minister in two significant ministries, all in the space of five years. And now here I was gunning for deputy leader of the party. Even without my association with Golding, this would have evoked some chagrin.

But I followed that path because I saw things that needed to be done, I felt that I could do them, and I went after positions that would give me the necessary authority to do so. My ambition was not to rise for the sake of gaining power, it was to be in positions where I could wield the influence to make the changes that I saw as necessary for the JLP to move forward.

When I decided to run for deputy leader for Area Council Four – the parishes of Hanover, Westmoreland, St James, St Elizabeth (where my constituency was) and Trelawny – it was because I perceived that the seats were floundering and in need of leadership. At the constituency level, the delegates were appealing for the party to listen to them and make some changes.

Horace Chang and I had a conversation in which he indicated to me that he was intending to retire from the deputy leader position to go for the chairmanship of the party. If he went on to the chairmanship, he told me, he saw me as a possible successor. So my initial decision to contest that position was taken and acted on entirely with Chang's blessing.

Having had that discussion with Chang, and getting calls from others in the Area Council, I decided to go for it. By then I was at a high point in my time in office, as the Ministry of Agriculture and Fisheries was perceived to be doing well with a fair bit of positive media publicity. The polls indicated that I was considered one of the top performers in the government. I was encouraged by many people to pursue the deputy leader position; they saw me as the right man for the job, and they saw that the position would further burnish my political standing.

Then Horace Chang changed his mind about going for the chairmanship. I came under pressure within the party to withdraw my candidacy. But by then I had done a lot of groundwork and met with many delegates and got a feel for the problems that the party was facing on the ground, and I was sure that I could address those issues effectively. I was already committed and I wasn't going to turn back.

The race was on. It took us through the five parishes. JLP people from outside the Area came to campaign on both sides. (Don Foote also contested the election, but did not have as much support.) The vigorous competition did have a positive spin-off in that it energized the base of the Area Council and provided an avenue for the delegates to get back in touch with the party leadership.

Here I was again, in a tense and tight internal leadership race. It was an intense contest and it was good for me in that it allowed me to understand and appreciate even more, the concerns, ideas and thoughts about the party itself and the changes being advocated. The delegates strongly expressed their feelings that the communication was amiss and that they wanted to be more involved in the decision-making process. That certainly wasn't a new problem, but that was the first time I was hearing these concerns from the source, and it was something that I committed myself to changing once I was in a position to do so.

The meeting where the voting took place at Green Island Primary School in Hanover was one of the largest Area Council meetings ever. Out of 1,250 delegates, 1,100 voted, which is virtually unprecedented for a JLP internal election. It was a peaceful day, but there were police everywhere, because of the potential for the scene turning ugly. I got 634 votes, to Horace Chang's 427, and Don Foote got the remainder.

Thus I entered the senior executive of the JLP, in an upset victory and on a tide of ill feelings that would linger for years to come. Once Horace Chang became general secretary of the party, and his goal was to steer the party to victory in the next election, we both found a way to be civil with each other in the interest of the party, even though the tension between us lingered. Some of his ardent supporters were not comfortable with my presence and were more open about their sentiments.

When we discussed the 2011 general election loss at executive committee meetings, Area Council Four leadership – meaning me – was blamed for the JLP losing the West. It was an unfair criticism: we did lose the West, but we lost everywhere else too, with no one region performing any better or worse than the other. Ironically, I think that the time that I spent working on area council matters could have contributed to the loss of the few votes I would have needed to retain my own seat in South West St Elizabeth in that election.

I would have preferred that my election as deputy leader of the JLP had not been so contentious, nor for the contention to have lingered on for so long. The need for a greater level of acceptance of the competitive practice of internal democracy within the JLP was again brought to the fore.

As much as we wrangled over the area council leadership race and the ensuing upset, those trials were nothing in comparison to the upheavals that awaited us just a few months later.

27

RESHUFFLE

Only a few months after the area council elections, in June 2011, Prime Minister Golding reshuffled the Cabinet. I was never consulted as to the thinking behind the reshuffle – nor did I expect to be consulted – but it was clear that the prime minister perceived that some people were not performing and he wanted to make some adjustments which would help to achieve some of the targets the administration had set. I was re-assigned from the Ministry of Agriculture and Fisheries to the Ministry of Trade and Industry.

I never requested to be put at Trade and Industry, and I was not immediately happy with the change. Ironically, this probably would have been my ministry of choice in the first round of appointments in 2007, had I had any say in the matter.

By this time, however, had it been up to me I would have stayed at Agriculture and Fisheries. I had a great team; we were accomplishing our goals and making real progress. But I accepted it because this was what the prime minister wanted, and it wasn't my place to question or challenge him.

I again found myself in a situation where the perception was that my appointment was an indication that I was one of Golding's 'favoured ones'. Having had no discussion with Golding about it, and not having had any other sign from him that he considered me favoured, the most I can assume is that he thought I was doing a good job at Agriculture and

Fisheries and that I would continue to perform satisfactorily at another ministry.

Though this was a new ministry for me, many of the issues were similar to those we dealt with at Agriculture and Fisheries. I was determined to make the best of my time there. My academic training was in business and my doctoral research was perfectly suited to this ministry's mandate, and I was excited by the new challenge. There was still a learning curve that was time and energy consuming – time and energy that, in retrospect, had I been able to spend in my constituency, I probably wouldn't have lost in the elections that occurred shortly thereafter.

The topic of the day was 'Brand Jamaica' – the idea that our image and our culture are our greatest assets, our best possibility for us to move forward as a nation. This was a concept that I had recognized early, from my days as a graduate student in Georgia in the 1990s, and which was reinforced when I was at the Ministry of Agriculture and Fisheries.

The branding of our goods and services is key for the future of agriculture, for tourism, and for virtually everything we wish to sell to the world. In agriculture, we simply can't compete in commodities markets, but we have a competitive edge when it comes to branded niche market products, especially and including foods and condiments.

On a per capita basis, Jamaica is one of the most recognized countries in the world. We have an outsized reputation, given the size of our population, our landmass, and our economy. Our reputation in athletics, music, as manufacturers of some of the world's most famous rums and coffees, among other claims to fame, have led to a powerful brand that we have yet to fully capitalize on.

Those of us who have travelled overseas will likely have experienced what it is like to be recognized as a Jamaican.

For most of us, once people recognize that we are Jamaican – and people often pick up on our accent immediately – they usually are curious about us and also friendly towards us. It is usually a positive experience to be identified as a Jamaican outside of Jamaica.

What is it about Jamaicans that makes us special? I do believe we are special, though that is perhaps my own nationalistic pride and sentiment. When I was at the Ministry of Agriculture and Fisheries I asked for a study that showed that the flavour profile of many of our well-known products actually is better than comparable products because of their chemical makeup. We had some agricultural products tested, and the results showed that Jamaican products like ginger, thyme, and escallion are more concentrated in the flavours than similar products from other countries. So when we say Jamaican coffee tastes better than other coffee, it is more than just a nationalistic or sentimental proclamation. We can be confident that the assertion is based on the scientific fact that the taste buds enjoy it more than other coffees. The same goes for our honey, and many of our other products. There *is* something special about being Jamaican, at least in some things.

We have not, however, figured out how to capitalize on this. In February 2013, the world was abuzz over an advertisement by the German automobile manufacturer Volkswagen, when they featured a white American from Minnesota speaking with a Jamaican accent. This showed the global reach of the positive perception of Jamaica, regardless of the product, the manufacturer and the market having nothing to do with Jamaica itself.

We have other challenges: there are productivity issues that bedevil our agriculture and manufacturing efforts, issues that we have been grappling with for decades, as I had researched and written about over ten years before in my master's thesis.

Many of these issues are deeply rooted in our history and our culture, and we remain challenged to understand them in a way that will allow us to do what is necessary to change and become more productive.

There continue to be problems related to inefficient bureaucracy, which is a particular barrier when it comes to everyday tasks that businesses have to do like registering a company, obtaining necessary licenses, and paying taxes. We talk about fixing these problems, and incremental steps are taken here and there, yet we don't see any dramatic results coming from the changes.

I had dozens of ideas that I set about implementing immediately. But my time at the ministry was never smooth, the time was too short, and it came far too late in the political cycle to register any tangible achievements. I was not there long enough to iron out the kinks that accompany any such transition, nor long enough to see any results from any of the initiatives that we started.

I didn't know this at the time, though. No one, least of all I, expected that the party and the country would be thrown into political uncertainty when Golding resigned just a few months later.

28

RESIGNATION

Just three months after the Cabinet reshuffle, on September 25, 2011, Bruce Golding announced his resignation as prime minister of Jamaica. He had wanted to resign from earlier in the year, after the Manatt Enquiry failed to adequately clear him in the public's perception of wrongdoing in the Christopher 'Dudus' Coke extradition saga.

The Manatt, Phelps and Phillips Enquiry, also known as the Dudus/Manatt Enquiry, commenced in January 2011 to investigate the circumstances surrounding the handling of the United States of America's extradition request for Coke, an alleged drug lord and supposed strongman of Golding's West Kingston constituency.

Golding's initial refusal to comply with the extradition request, the Jamaica Labour Party's (JLP's) engagement of a Washington law firm to lobby the US government on its behalf in the matter, and the subsequent May 2010 incursion into Tivoli Gardens to capture Coke once the government did go ahead with attempting to fulfil the extradition request, had all brought huge criticism of Golding from every corner of the society.

Golding had hoped that the enquiry would present his case as he saw it – that he had done nothing wrong. But the outcome was more nuanced, and because it wasn't clear-cut, his detractors, and especially the People's National Party

(PNP) public relations machine, were able to maintain the impression to the public that he was guilty.

His resignation, when it happened, was not a surprise to me or many of us in the JLP. Golding had become increasingly withdrawn and diffident about his ability to lead the party into victory in the next election. We (the party senior executive together with Golding) had agreed to do some research into Golding's winnability in the next election, and that he would make his decision based on the focus group findings.

The research found that Golding's image and credibility were badly damaged, but not beyond repair. Golding felt the effort would not be worthwhile, the outcome too uncertain, and he used the study to justify his decision to step down. I don't think it mattered what the poll said, Golding had made up his mind. He would have interpreted any poll result as a reason to resign, regardless of the report's analysis and conclusions.

Though we understood the reasoning behind his decision, none of us actually expected Golding to go through with it. Jamaican politicians seldom resign, even in the most glaring of scandals. Much more pressure was brought to bear on Seaga for a much longer time before he finally stepped down.

Golding's decision further reinforced his position as an outlier in the historical characterization of the typical Jamaican politician. While Michael Manley and P.J. Patterson resigned as prime ministers, it was because they were retiring, and to facilitate a peaceful internal party leadership transition. Hugh Shearer was a notable exception to the Jamaican political party trajectory of resignations when he went quietly, bowing to the requests of senior JLP members, and stepped down as leader of the opposition after the JLP's loss to the PNP in 1972.

Bruce Golding genuinely had a vision for Jamaica – a vision that was realistic, necessary and, with the right wind, doable. And he worked tirelessly to have that vision implemented. I truly believe he wanted to make a positive difference, and in many areas he did. He has a concrete and comprehensive grasp of the issues facing Jamaica, and coupled with his political experience, and his foray into the National Democratic Movement (NDM), there are few other people in Jamaica who understand Jamaica the way he does.

He was the right man for the job when he was elected in 2007. The JLP made no mistake in supporting his return to the party and his ascendance to leader. Golding was the man who substantially delivered an election victory after seven successive defeats at the polls (between local and general elections) for the JLP. For all those reasons – the content, the experience, the electability – it would be unfair and misplaced for anyone to suggest otherwise.

Where Golding became his own worst enemy was how he approached governance. He spoke about broadening representation, but spent too much time micromanaging. Seaga's greatest weakness was also Golding's – a penchant for being involved with the minute details of the policy process and the day-to-day work of getting things done. He was bogged down by tiny tasks that precluded him seeing and working on bigger picture issues. The weaknesses of his approach were an unintended by-product of his management style and personality. He did not set out to alienate people, or to be a micromanager.

He was working 18-hour days, but he wasn't getting 18 hours worth of work done. The way he was operating was not sustainable – it was not possible to maintain control over the government and strengthen the party with his approach. Like Seaga, Golding did not trust others enough to delegate real responsibility to them, even if the distrust had different sources: for Seaga it was his autocratic personality, for Golding it was a perceived lack of capacity or effectiveness of those around him. There was a sense that he never really had faith in the people in the JLP, or they him, and that they merely saw him as a winning ticket, and in return they thought he saw them as his vehicle to prime minister.

He had spoken about Belmont Road (JLP Headquarters) right after the election and it not being abandoned. Yet, when he became PM that is exactly what happened. He allowed the party to fall to the side, and the party weakened and drifted. In retrospect, he should have undertaken a concerted effort to build on the victory immediately after the election, and properly heal some of the deep divisions in the party that had been festering for decades. But he didn't have the time or capacity to do it himself, and there was no one else who could do it. Inevitably, the party continued to fracture.

His judgment errors climaxed with the Manatt-Tivoli debacle. We all make mistakes, but many of us are saved from making fatal errors by the input of others, who point out our mistakes before they are detrimental. Because he didn't let people in, Golding didn't benefit from other points of view at critical points in his decision-making about Dudus and the extradition request. In the Manatt-Tivoli situation, Golding relied too much on his own interpretation and opinion and acted without sufficient adherence to the counsel of others, and he erred gravely in his judgment.

I was not intensely involved at any stage, nor was I privy to the inner details of the discussions related to Dudus or Manatt. It didn't cross any portfolio that I had any involvement in, and apart from a few informal discussions, I had little to do with it.

I don't believe that Bruce Golding intended to deceive anyone, not least the Jamaican people, nor to cover anything up. He was in an invidious position and he believed he was acting on principle. He felt he had a genuine duty to protect the right of a Jamaican citizen and, in this case, a member of his constituency.

His decision to be at the frontline of the government's position, involving a controversial member of his constituency was a poor one. A better approach would have been to allow the attorney general and the courts to handle it. Similarly, his presentation in Parliament which ramped up the rhetoric around the Americans and their embassy was unnecessary and provocative and drew battle lines that he could hardly expect to win over.

The PNP did an excellent job in using the Manatt issue to hammer Golding and the JLP for political gain – nothing unexpected there. But it came at a steep price, not only for Golding but for the country. The discussions and eventually the enquiry were not about a search for truth, but more about theatrics and a move for political advantage.

The PNP succeeded in their mission to damage Golding, though he provided the ammunition. Golding opted for the enquiry because he saw it as an opportunity to redeem himself. If he hadn't gone through with the enquiry, he would have been accused of a cover-up, and he genuinely did not believe he had done anything wrong. He did not have much of a choice – whatever path he took, he could not avoid damaging consequences.

The Manatt episode brought to the fore the paradoxes of Bruce Golding. He is an incredibly bright person, one of the most intelligent men I have ever known. Yet his views as they came to be expressed via the Manatt crisis were parochial and myopic. For someone who understood Jamaica so well, he didn't seem to grasp Jamaica's place in today's world, particularly vis-à-vis the US.

He misread how Jamaicans viewed the US. Jamaica is their home and Jamaicans are proud of their country, but America still represents their route to economic progress, and Jamaicans are loathe to do anything that might jeopardize their own personal access to the US, whether as migrants, tourists, or exporters.

The incursion into West Kingston in search of Coke bruised Golding's image and reputation, as it did Jamaica's in the international community. Golding himself seemed to have felt troubled by the lack of clarity on who the victims of the Tivoli incursion were – were they criminals, as the security forces claimed? Or innocents, as the human rights activists insisted?

The Dudus–Manatt mess had a huge impact on Golding. It was clear to me that he felt abandoned by the party and by society at large. He was being hammered from outside and not being sufficiently supported from within the party. He was made to feel as if he were a liability to the party as opposed to when he first returned and represented the JLP's only hope.

From what I could see, he had made up his mind to resign months before the announcement. He was withdrawn. He would drop hints about it. He seemed depressed, and hopeless about regaining the trust and confidence of the Jamaican people. Resigning was his last hope at redemption, the most honourable thing he could do.

Once we began to realize the gravity of the situation, and especially how deeply he had internalized his failure, a group of people, myself included, met with him to discuss his political future. There were some who encouraged him to stay on and others who didn't encourage so strongly.

My own position was that he should stay. I felt that there was over a year to go before an election was due, and we had the time to repair some of the damage to his approval ratings and the party's support. The economy was showing signs of improvement, but the country's economic situation was very delicate. Crime was trending down as there was a dramatic 40 per cent drop in the murder rate after the Tivoli incursion. Golding was still the best person to lead the party and the country; in my view he was the best leader at the time, albeit one who had made a terrible series of mistakes.

Once Golding resigned, the initial transition to Andrew Holness as the party's new leader was superficially smooth, but internally the JLP was still weak. If it seemed too good to be true, it was. That weakness would soon come to the surface and prove to be our downfall in a very short space of time.

29

PRIME MINISTER HOLNESS

The discussion about who would succeed Golding began immediately – within hours of Golding's announcement that Sunday afternoon. I found the feverish haste premature and distasteful, but perhaps it should be expected in the Jamaican – or any – political context.

Golding made what must have been the most difficult decision of his political life, a life that was already replete with its share of dramatic events. His mother had just passed, and he was grieving; I had just been through a similar situation, so I identified. Left to me, I would have given him some time to mourn his mother and his decision before we started talking about who was to succeed him. But politics waits for no man, and I was in the minority in thinking that way.

My name came up as a possible contender, as did Audley Shaw, Andrew Holness, and Dr Ken Baugh. I quickly came to the conclusion that I was not going to put myself forward. I knew I could lead the party effectively if I were put in the position, but I made no indication that I was going for it. Not because I was relatively new to politics, and not because I was relatively new to the JLP, even though this would have been a formidable obstacle, as I did not enjoy the confidence of the inner sanctum of the party. My gut told me that it wasn't the right time for me. Though the polls considered me to have a good chance at being the next leader, and many people encouraged me to declare myself a contender, my main concern was who would be the best prospect to lead the party, and what could I do to facilitate a peaceful and productive transition. That person was not going to be me.

Initially, I felt Audley Shaw would be a good candidate because of his considerable experience in national politics, his seniority in the party, his favourable standing in the polls, and his experience at the Ministry of Finance. Audley Shaw is a natural leader, is charismatic, and has an excellent connection with people.

Andrew Holness had a good track record in his ministry, and he was from an under-represented age cohort in the context of a party structure where leadership renewal was lacking. His public standing and his winnability weighed heavily in his favour. Also, importantly, Golding made it clear that he wanted Andrew Holness to be party leader. In hindsight, one might even speculate that Golding had Holness succeeding him in mind since 2008 when he appointed him leader of government business in the Parliament.

Ultimately, after thinking it through, discussing it with people I trusted, and weighing everything, I felt Holness was the best person to take the baton at that time. I had a discussion with him and told him what I thought and gave him my support. I also told Audley Shaw my decision and encouraged him to join me in supporting Andrew Holness.

Many in the party came to the same conclusion, in one way or another, and what we experienced was something few would have expected of the JLP – a transition of power from one leader to another that was devoid of fractiousness, contention, and drama. It was a remarkable moment for the JLP, and made me proud of the party.

Andrew Holness was encouraged, immediately on taking office, to call an election. The ghost of Portia Simpson Miller and her experience when she first became prime minister haunted him. Everywhere he turned people besieged him to not make the mistake Portia did, which was to not capitalize on the bump in the popularity that she got immediately after she became prime minister, and call an election right away.

But there was more to the haste – there were economic challenges on the horizon that many felt would be best tackled with a renewed mandate. The economic situation was dire and difficult decisions were ahead of us in order to balance the budget. The thinking was that Andrew Holness and the JLP would not survive the fallout of the 'bitter medicine' that whichever party was in power would have to administer to prevent a complete collapse of the economy, particularly in the context of a stalemate with the International Monetary Fund (IMF) that had lingered for over a year. Better to have an election before having to take the extreme measures, and once back in office for another term, do what had to be done.

All of that made sense at the time, but in hindsight it was clear that the JLP was just not ready for an election. The party was weak and had been for a long time, and the transition though on the surface smooth, had left considerable disgruntlement particularly among the delegates and party workers. We were nowhere near in campaign mode. Most of us who would have been candidates had mistakenly counted on having another year and had not been on the ground. Seats that didn't have candidates were hurriedly filled. People were hastily recruited, many of them complete newcomers to politics, and they were not adequately prepared or supported to contest their seats.

Added to that, we misread the enumeration statistics. There had been a spike in the enumeration numbers, and we thought that our supporters were among that spike, but we were wrong. It was the PNP that had been doing the groundwork and enumerating thousands of their own young supporters, while we had done nothing.

Holness found himself backed into a corner by promising an election before the end of the year, 2011. It would come to be his greatest mistake during his short time as prime minister, as we would soon realize. Our stocks fell precipitously once the election was called.

Our campaign was ineffective, and we did not have the time to see that and correct it. We put together a manifesto that attested to our achievements against our commitments, yet the manifesto did not feature sufficiently in the campaign. The issue was not our record; it was our communication of the record. The JLP failed to adequately convey to the Jamaican people what we had done while in office.

Yet we had done a lot and achieved a great deal. In our 2007–2011 term in office, the policies we pursued and implemented yielded marked improvements in many aspects of Jamaicans' quality of life. Murder and serious crime were reduced by double-digit percentages, and the Jamaica Constabulary Force began a much-needed process of reforming itself and reducing internal corruption and inefficiency.

The economy was stabilized and the foundations were established for the economy to finally realize some growth, after decades of stagnation. We divested entities that had been losing billions of dollars of taxpayers' money, and most of the entities were sold as going concerns, so there was little fallout in terms of job losses. We achieved a lowering of the interest rate, a stabilization of the exchange rate, and a low inflation rate. We implemented the Jamaica Debt Exchange (JDX), which allowed for a desperately needed restructuring of our onerous debt burden. The JDX was unprecedented in Jamaica's history, and was so successful that it became a model for debt restructuring programmes around the world.

The JLP administration's policies of removing hospital user fees for all Jamaicans, doubling the benefits available through the Programme of Advancement through Health and Education (PATH – a social safety net programme), and adding over 100,000 people to the programme, improving the water supply, and restructuring informal settlements, directly improved the lives of hundreds of thousands of people. The policies that we pursued in the agriculture and tourism sectors saw growth and improved productivity, greater employment, and greater returns for investors in those sectors, even in the face of the global recession.

But our campaign failed to communicate any of that effectively, nor other positive aspects of the party and what we had to offer Jamaica. We did not showcase the new women candidates who were running for the JLP. Never has any political party in Jamaica had such a fantastic pool of young women, all accomplished professionals, running for national office. The narrow margins that they lost by were testament to how strong their candidacies were, and that perhaps with just a little more support and guidance they could have been victorious.

Had we given these women candidates, and the other newcomers, more resources, and highlighted them more in the national campaign, I am sure we could have turned around the perception that was both within and outside the party that they were opportunists just put there for their looks and profile. Even if we still lost the election, had they won they would have gained valuable experience as first-term MPs.

These were just a few of many mistakes we made that accounted for our loss in 2011.

And I lost my seat, which contributed to the overall loss of the party, 42–21, a massive defeat, by any measure. It was an upset when I won the seat and an upset when I lost, but I knew exactly what had gone wrong.

30

Thirteen Votes

Going into the election I knew I was weaker than I had been in the 2007 election, significantly so. I was not as comfortable in a prospective victory as I would have liked. Danny Buchanan's son Hugh, a former school sportsmaster, was the People's National Party (PNP) candidate-caretaker, and he drew on his father's political base, and on the well-organized PNP election machinery, to mobilize PNP core supporters to come out.

By the time the polls closed on election day, I suspected things were not going my way. The media reported first that I had lost the South West St Elizabeth seat, then that I had won. But I knew even after the seat had been declared for me on election night, after the preliminary count, that the story was not over.

On election day ballots are counted at the polling station and returned to the ballot box; the box is sealed and the numbers are written on each box. The numbers on the outside of the boxes are added up at the central counting location, and that is the result that is given to the media and used to call a seat on election night.

On election night it was declared that I had won by 110 votes, but that number did not square with the numbers reported by the indoor agents who had been tallying at the polling stations, so I knew something was amiss. The PNP would have known that too. It was clear that the result was not final, and there was a disturbing sense of unresolvedness.

I went to Black River Primary School, where the ballot boxes were coming in, to check on my workers and do what I could to keep people calm. But my supporters were agitated, and so were Buchanan's. Rumours began to circulate that ballots had been stolen and boxes had been stuffed. Tension was high.

Neither group knew whether to celebrate or go home, and the uncertainty was destabilizing for everyone. The police thought it prudent to station a detail at my house overnight. I called my lawyers that night and asked them to come to St. Elizabeth first thing the next morning. The goal was to be prepared for any eventuality.

Despite the turmoil, and the uncertainty over the outcome, after a few drinks I got a good night's sleep. I was confident in the process, regardless of whether I won or lost. I knew, and the people close to me knew, how hard I had worked, and of my dedication to the constituency and my constituents. But given the discrepancy in the numbers between the indoor agents' tally and what was reported by the central counting location, and given the large swing against the JLP at the national level, I braced myself for an unfavourable outcome.

The next morning my three lawyers – Lorna Bennett from Saint Elizabeth and Floyd Green and Wentworth Charles from Kingston – arrived to attend the two-day count. They observed as each ballot was counted, which ultimately resulted in a 13-vote difference in favour of the PNP's Hugh Buchanan. We all agreed that it would not be worth the effort to try to overturn that result.

Some people felt I conceded too quickly and too easily, but it was the right thing to do then, and I have never regretted it. Separate from my conviction that the result was correct, I did not want to be a part of a process that would continue the uncertainty and generate animosity. I spared the constituents and the nation what would likely have been a futile ordeal.

I knew why I had lost, even after my convincing victory in 2007, and after all the work I did in the constituency. There were many reasons, each playing their own role in chipping away at my support, and weighing the balance in favour of the PNP.

I analysed the numbers, right down to each of the 96 polling divisions (PDs) in the constituency. I looked at the votes that were canvassed before the election, the votes I thought I had. In strategizing for election day, the candidates and their teams looked at the voters' list and saw who they thought would vote, and for whom. The party workers who live in the areas and know the people personally make their educated guesses.

After the election we did an audit. We compared the canvas to the actual votes cast. We realized that there was a large gap between what we had canvassed and the numbers of voters on the day. Many people who would have voted for me had not gone to the polls at all. A large proportion of our core, known supporters had stayed home. This was a serious failure. It is one thing for 'maybes' to not vote, or to appear to have voted for the other party, but when your core support doesn't vote, this is a critical problem. They were disgruntled about how the constituency level-campaign had progressed, they were reacting to interpersonal differences with other party workers or members, and some of them were simply influenced by the national swing against the JLP.

The fact that the constituency is a nearly three-hour drive from Kingston placed me at a disadvantage, as did the physical/geographical size of the area. I was very involved in my ministerial work, and couldn't get to the constituency as often as I would have liked. In smaller urban constituencies, a candidate or MP can leave office and be there in less than an hour. In some constituencies, she or he can walk the entire constituency in just a few hours, stopping to talk to people along the way.

Some of the work I had done in my capacity as minister of agriculture and fisheries, such as changing the regulations to protect the island's fisheries, worked against me. One of the no-fish zones that had been established fell within the boundaries of my constituency. The new rules changed the size of the holes in the fish pot nets to let the smaller fish swim out, as part of the thrust towards more sustainable fishing. This may have angered up to a thousand fisherfolk who counted among my constituents.

The timing of the election was a factor. The Dudus–Manatt fiasco was still fresh in people's minds, and the new leadership of the party had not had enough time to erase that stain from people's memories. The election date, right after Christmas, was inconvenient for many people. Some people were not even in the constituency where they were registered, as they were away visiting friends and family, as people do during the holidays.

There was also a perception, not just in my constituency, but nationally, that the JLP didn't care enough about the hardships that people were facing. The conventional wisdom was that Holness as prime minister had warned of 'bitter medicine' to come, but had not given an accompanying message of hope that the medicine would yield any improvement. It was another lesson in the perils of telling the people the truth and getting punished for it.

Throughout the country, the PNP successfully mobilized its core support, many of whom had stayed home in 2007. The voter turnout for the JLP was 405, 234 in 2011, while in 2007 it was 410, 438. So some five thousand fewer people voted for the JLP in 2011. The PNP counted 463, 232 votes in 2011, compared to 405, 293 in 2007 – nearly 60,000 more people turned out to vote for the PNP.

Most JLP supporters who voted for me in 2007 did so again in 2011, save a few (a critical few, as it turned out), but the PNP, determined to unseat me, worked extremely hard to galvanize their support and get their voters to the polling stations. Hugh Buchanan had a team that ran an effective campaign and got their supporters out on election day. Hugh was not favoured to win the seat, and he was a newcomer to politics. All things considered, he did well.

I take full responsibility for my loss, even after I take into account all these factors. The seat has a relatively equal number of core supporters for both parties, and I simply did not do enough to get my core support out, while the PNP went to extraordinary lengths, as is their right and their obligation. Even though I had a strong team doing work in the constituency, and I had the results to prove it, I myself wasn't there, and people wanted and expected to see me. I was not able to maintain the expectations that I myself had established in the run-up to 2007, after I won the seat.

Before I won the South West St Elizabeth seat, I made myself known by my presence; once I had won it, I continued to work for the people of the constituency by promoting development at many different levels, but I no longer had time to literally hold each and every hand. This was a key factor in my losing the seat. Jamaicans like to see their candidates, and sit with them in a rum bar, and have them visit during times of bereavement. The Don Anderson poll that I privately commissioned after the 2011 loss found that a key factor to my regaining the seat would be a greater level of interaction with the electorate in the constituency, more visibility, and generally more contact with the people.

These expectations of a candidate's constant presence in the constituency, even at events and activities that are more symbolic than productive, are core aspects of the paternalistic nature of Jamaican politics. The way that Jamaican politics has evolved the politician is held up as the ubiquitous problem-solver and caregiver, sponsor of sports competitions, and provider of jobs, food, housing, and school fees.

This style of politics may work in favour of new candidates eager to please and hungry to win, who have limitless time and energy to expend, but this is not a realistic option for candidates who are elected to office, and who take their jobs as ministers seriously. Furthermore, there is not very much meaningful work that can be done in this manner.

This populist politics that we practise will never move Jamaica forward in any real way. The dependency of constituent on politician, and the cycle of promises, cannot and do not amount to a political system that will ever bring us sustainable democratic social and economic development. At some point we all – politicians, political activists, party workers, voter-constituents – have to come to terms with these uncomfortable facts, and begin the process of changing them.

When I lost the seat in 2011, after the initial shock and upset dissipated, my wife Neadene was actually happy and relieved, as she realized what life without politics would mean for us and our family. For the first time in years, I would have time and energy to spend with her and the children. They are the ones who have sacrificed the most for my political career.

There are many would-be politicians, men and women, who do not pursue their interest or potential because they are not willing to sacrifice their families to their long absences, or their personal lives to the overwhelming demands of a political career. A cursory look at the successful politicians in Jamaica will reveal that they either have grown children, no children at all, or have partners who shoulder the entire parental responsibility. Choosing to contribute to one's country via representative politics should not preclude being an engaged parent.

As we mature politically, we need to reflect on the all-consuming nature of the way we do politics, and ask ourselves if this is really what we want for our leaders and ourselves. We need a cultural change in the nature of our politics, more than de-tribalization, we need to de-paternalize how we do politics in Jamaica. How we go about adjusting constituents' expectations has to be something that we all – political parties, delegates and other representatives, and constituents and citizens – would have to discuss and agree on. It would have to be a discussion that occurs outside the realm of partisan politics, an authentic dialogue about how we are all going to make Jamaican politics more effective and truly representative.

Things move quickly after an election in Jamaica. It is remarkable, when one considers the logistics and the number of people involved, the speed at which an outgoing administration vacates office and the incoming party takes up its mark. Just one week after the election, I had moved out of my government-assigned house and cleared my desk at the ministry. All that remained was to answer the question: what next?

31

AGONY AND DEFEAT

I didn't wait for the dust to settle after the 2011 election. The very morning after the election when I knew I had lost the seat and the Jamaica Labour Party (JLP) had lost the election, I began to think about what I would do next. I was still the candidate-caretaker for the constituency, but I also needed to provide for my family, and I had no choice but to move on to new things.

In the midst of my urgency to move forward, I allowed myself some time and mental space to reflect on the past few years, to think about what I might do in the years ahead, and to make some decisions. I wanted to fully understand and absorb what my losing the seat meant for me and for my future in Jamaican politics.

The idea for this book was one outcome of that thought process, as I felt that my reflections were not just about my personal life and choices, but also about how they are shaped by the political system, and by the broader Jamaican sociocultural context. I felt that exploring my own evolution as a politician and a person might give me some insight into the system itself, as well as to my rightful place in it.

I commissioned a poll to help me to better understand what had happened in the South West St Elizabeth election. I took the emotion out of it and looked at it scientifically. The poll mainly looked at the perceptions of the voters in my constituency, and it showed that I was popular in the constituency and that I had high approval ratings for my work as MP.

Over 70 per cent of the people polled agreed that I had worked hard in the constituency, that I had a good relationship with people in the constituency, that I was a good listener, that they had expected me to retain the seat, and that I should run again. The poll attributed my failures largely to the constituency management team around me, the national issues that bedevilled the JLP, and to my low visibility in the constituency.

I shouldn't have needed a poll to tell me this. I should have recognized these weaknesses before the election and fixed them. I don't blame anyone but myself for the loss. Once I had this objective analysis in hand, I quickly came to terms with the loss of the seat, and took the important lessons from it. It was a genuine loss and I was sure of that. I didn't need to do a magisterial recount because my lawyers had advised me that there was nothing to be gained from it. I lost fair and square.

I felt that I had done my best in my time at the Ministry of Agriculture and Fisheries, and even though I barely got out the blocks at the Ministry of Industry and Commerce, I had no regrets about my time there.

I came to terms with all that had happened; the questions were more about what lay ahead. I considered my own career, both in and out of politics. Where was I in terms of the goals, I had for myself in my public and professional life? I thought about my public policy and representation roles. Was I doing the right thing? Was I having any impact? Was I in the right place for what my ambitions were?

Of course, I had to think about my personal and family life. My first order of business was to reconnect with my wife and children. I had to devote a great deal of time and energy to my family, and to strengthen my bond with them. My children and wife missed me, and I missed them. Between the 2011 election and the 2016 election, I spent more time with them than I ever have, and it was time well spent.

I drove the children to school, got involved in their schoolwork, took them on outings, and I was home with them in the evenings. We regularly had meals together, something that seldom happened when I was in office or campaigning.

My next order of business was to earn a living and shore up my family's finances. I had spent most of my adult life in politics, and while in office I was living in a government house that I had only a few days to vacate. I had limited savings and no foreign bank accounts to fall back on. Neadene and I had a business in May Pen, but I wanted to ensure that we would never again have to deal with the financial uncertainty that had hovered on the edges of our lives the previous years.

I considered a few job offers, and explored some business possibilities. I knew I couldn't go to a nine-to-five – after academia and then being a minister I just didn't have it in me to be constrained to an office job. I didn't consider going back to The University of the West Indies, though I hadn't ruled out teaching completely.

I restructured the May Pen business by expanding its product line. I re-registered the consultancy practice I had before active politics, and began a start-up with a friend. I considered myself blessed because I was able to solidly embark on this process of rebuilding within the first six months of my election loss, and the early results of those efforts were encouraging. By mid-2012, I was in a job, a director of seven different private sector entities, co-owner of a new business venture, and consultant on a number of overseas and local assignments.

My main occupation was on the UWI Mona campus, though not in an academic position. The opportunity arose for me to join the Caribbean Policy and Research Institute (CaPRI), a public policy think tank based at the university. I had known about CaPRI and its mission to promote policy dialogue and reform through empirical research. CaPRI's genesis was an independent study group called 'Taking Responsibility', led by John Rapley, who at the time was a political science lecturer in the Department of Government, and comprised of academics from UWI, including Professor Alvin Wint, business people like Wayne Chen, a few politicians such as Imani Duncan, and people working in public policy planning and development such as then-head of the Planning Institute of Jamaica (PIOJ), Dr Wesley Hughes.

For two years, 2005–2007, they conducted research and workshops trying to understand why the Jamaican economy had performed so poorly since independence. They found, as was to be expected, that the answer was multi-dimensional, but two things stood out: the unwillingness of Jamaica and especially its leaders to own up to our problems and take responsibility for their creation and resolution, and the absence of reliable data to inform policy decisions.

When the Taking Responsibility project ended, many of the people who were involved and who knew of the work wanted it to continue. Initially, the Private Sector Organisation of Jamaica (PSOJ) was to have hosted it, but Gordon Shirley who was then the principal at UWI offered it a home on the Mona campus.

CaPRI's goal is to address the absence of data-driven policy decisions by conducting research into issues related to economic growth and development and to make policy recommendations based on that research, as well as to share the findings of their research with the different players and stakeholders involved in those particular issues, as well as with the broader community.

I have been interested in how policy is formulated and implemented since I did my master's degree, and that was the topic of my doctoral thesis. CaPRI's interests were aligned with my own interests, experience, and skills.

CaPRI would be an ideal place for me to apply what I had learnt over the past five years, and to think through many of the problems still confronting Jamaica, and what the policy solutions might be. CaPRI took me on as co-executive director, along with Dr Damien King, an economist at UWI Mona, who was a member of the founding Taking Responsibility group.

I found myself back on the Mona campus of the University, engaged in the exciting work of policy research on a wide range of issues that are germane to Jamaican and Caribbean development. Many of these issues I had come face to face with during my time in government, and now I had the experience and knowledge of having been involved in the real world of policy implementation. I was brought on board to raise funds and increase CaPRI's advocacy activities, and coordinate topical research projects. We achieved many of our goals.

CaPRI had already done some important work before I joined, such as its research on Informal Investment Schemes, which informed the government's decision not to bail out the investors who lost millions of dollars in Cash Plus, Olint, and the other Ponzi-type schemes that had proliferated in 2008.

At CaPRI, I didn't face the demands of being in government and the political pressures that can often interfere with objective decision-making, but my experience in government and politics helped me to understand them, and that understanding contributed to my informed interpretation of our research results and make more realistic policy recommendations in our reports.

There were people who openly expressed their doubts that I was the right person for the CaPRI job, because of my political affiliation, as well as many, I am sure, who thought it but never said it outright. In the US and other countries, it is standard practice for active politicians to do stints in academia and in think tanks when their party is not in office. It is a positive cycle of real-life experience informing policy and policy informing what actually happens.

I appreciate that the CaPRI board took a chance on me. In a country where partisan lines can run so deep, it is unusual to take on a person whose political allegiances are so clearly stated. We are not accustomed to active politicians being able to put their partisan affiliations aside and think independently. It shows that we are maturing as a democracy. It was also an invaluable learning experience for me at the same time as it allowed me to continue in public service.

CaPRI continued this precedent by appointing former People's National Party (PNP) Senator Imani Duncan-Price to my position when I left CaPRI after winning a seat in the 2016 election and being appointed to the Cabinet. Duncan-Price was an ideal candidate for the job, not only because of her outstanding academic qualifications and her earlier experience as a founding member of CaPRI, but also because of her own experience in politics and in government, as a senator and a candidate for Member of Parliament.

The offer of the CaPRI job – and the other offers that came my way – suggested to me that my own personal efforts to move beyond tribal politics had been effective. I was encouraged that there were people who perceived me as being able to manage the transition from politics to business and academia and bring my training and experience to the job in a non-partisan way.

In my time at CaPRI, together with Damien King, the organization led a number of research initiatives that have had an impact on public policy. The Caribbean Development Bank sponsored a study on debt in the English-speaking Caribbean countries, examining the debt profile and making policy recommendations for Caribbean governments. The study's results and recommendations were the basis of discussions at the national, regional, and international level, and informed presentations given internationally by then-Minister of Finance, Dr Peter Phillips, and then-Prime Minister, Portia Simpson Miller.

CaPRI's policy brief on urban waste management that was released in 2015 spoke directly to the problems at Kingston's Riverton City Dump. The CaPRI report directly informed the changes that were made in the aftermath of the week-long fire that brought the capital to a standstill in March 2015.

I also got involved in other endeavours, including a number of board positions in private sector companies. Some of those directorships then developed into larger ventures. The most significant was a US$500-million project for the construction of a UWI campus in Montego Bay plus a Tech Park and housing. The agreement for the project was signed in May 2014 between Barnett Limited Tech Park, Gore Homes, and the University.

In my various capacities as a consultant, think tank director, board director and businessperson, I worked with people across different sectors, private and public, including government agencies and even ministries, on policy issues that are germane to national development. Virtually everyone I worked with, including many people in the PNP government, was able to get past my political affiliation. Most people, it seems, were able to appreciate that I can and do wear other hats, and they trusted that I would perform, whether at CaPRI or elsewhere, without partisan considerations or influence, as I did.

Many other politicians do not have such a positive experience once they leave office. The lawyers do okay, they go back to their practice, but it's hard to go from being a minister back to a nine-to-five office job. This is another feature of our politics that I would like to see change. I hope that one day Jamaica's political climate will be practised in a way that allows its main actors to generate sufficient confidence in the wider societal context to be able to engage in other productive areas of life when they leave the political stage. The more we detribalize political activity and improve confidence in the political process, the more likely this will be the case.

Finally, I had to take care of my health. Politics as we practice it in Jamaica is detrimental to a person's health. There are few politicians who are able to maintain a healthy lifestyle while in office or campaigning. The amount of time spent on the road, whether travelling within the island or overseas, means that there is little opportunity for exercise, and no daily routine within which to eat healthy meals. I gained a lot of weight during my time in politics, and was very out of shape. It was a relief to have the time and space to reclaim my health.

I became a lot more health conscious. I started a fitness regime and got back to a healthy weight. One of the activities that brought me great joy in the year after leaving office was learning to swim with my youngest son, Adam. I was able to do something I had wanted to do since I was a child – learn to swim – and combine exercise with a fun, bonding activity with my child. I could never have done such a thing were I still in government.

It is ironic that having unexpectedly lost my seat by just 13 votes it could turn out to have brought so many positive benefits to my life. My time in government was fulfilling and challenging, but my time in private life was also rewarding, just in different ways. I didn't decelerate; I merely changed gears, while still moving steadily forward. I adjusted my mindset and everything else followed.

I was very fortunate that while I spent some of the most productive years of my life studying or in public service, I was able to get myself to a point where I did not need politics for my personal economic survival, nor did I need to be in politics to contribute to public service.

Even though I didn't have the foresight to plan for a life after politics, in part because I did not expect my political career to end so quickly or abruptly, I would suggest to anyone who ever considers getting into politics to always have a post-politics plan, financially, and career-wise.

I think key to my ability to transition as I did was that I always maintained my integrity in everything I did, including and especially when I was a minister. As Warren Buffet said, it takes 20 years to build a reputation and five minutes to ruin it. In everything I have done, I have sought to protect my reputation.

I have always treated people with respect, even if we were of different or even opposing views on a matter. In a country as small as Jamaica, you can be sure that you will continue crossing paths with people for years to come, and even if you disagree with someone, you still need to treat one another politely and graciously. I have maintained good relationships with almost everyone that I have interacted with, even when we were at odds.

Another important event occurred after I left office, one that I hadn't planned for or anticipated. An open question in my life was finally answered in 2012 when I met my father for the first time.

32

FATHER

I had started looking for my father when I was in high school. I learned his full name nearly ten years later. Another ten years after that I tried to contact him. Now it was ten years after that attempt where he rebuffed me. I never had a relationship with my stepfather during his short marriage to my mother, and while I was raised for a time by my grandfather and there were uncles involved in my upbringing, I had never formed a father-son relationship with anyone.

Through the efforts of a friend who insisted that I make another effort to connect with my father, I learned he is descended from a Peer (a member of the British nobility), that his family's roots were in France, and that among my antecedents were a member of the British House of Commons and a well-known English cricketer. My first thoughts on hearing all this were, perhaps that's where my political inclinations come from, and where my son Charles, who is an avid cricketer, gets his athletic abilities.

My friend tracked him down in England and gave him a file of printouts – newspaper articles and the like – about me and my political career. Not long afterwards, I got an email from him. He said he would see me, but only once. I had a trip to England coming up and we arranged to meet in London.

We met at a gentlemen's club where he was a member. These elitist members-only institutions have been around since the

1700s and most of them still maintain strict membership rules, including the exclusion of women members. I had never crossed paths with a member of one of these establishments, so this was my first time entering this supposedly hallowed preserve of the British aristocracy.

When I arrived I was shown to a private room. They were expecting me – he would have had to give them my name for me to gain entry. They offered me a drink, which I welcomed. I needed something to calm my nerves. I surprised myself with how nervous I was; I hadn't expected to feel anything, yet emotions I didn't even know I had were churning in my head and in my stomach.

Once he entered the room everything moved at lightning speed. He still had most of his hair, which I was glad to see. He had visited me shortly after I was born, he told me, but left Jamaica soon after. He then worked in other countries and around the UK as an engineer, settling down when he married and had two children – my half-siblings. He had not told his wife and children about me, even though the relationship with my mother, and my birth, long preceded them. His wife had not taken kindly to the revelation brought about by my friend's intervention, and that was problematic for him. His children still did not know about me and he wanted it to stay that way.

He asked me if I had felt deprived, growing up without a father, and I told him the truth – definitely not. He was very charitable about what he had learned about me, and encouraged me in my political career. I had simply wanted to meet him. I didn't want anything from him, except perhaps, for him to acknowledge me. I wasn't interested in any inheritance, nor in his title, nor in British citizenship.

Before I knew it we had talked for over three hours. When our meeting ended I felt that I was able to bring to a close an unfinished chapter in my life, having finally met the man who was responsible for bringing me into the world. As happy as my childhood was, as much as I might have never consciously felt like something was missing – or acknowledged that something was missing – there was something deep inside me that wanted to know for myself what the person whose genes I shared looked like. I wanted to make a connection, even if it was only a brief one.

While I had never knowingly felt a longing to know my father, when I did finally meet him, something clicked into place, and a sense of completeness that I didn't know wasn't there before, engulfed me. He got up to leave and told me I could stay as long as I wanted at the club. I walked him to the door. As we parted, he took a few steps, turned and took a long good look at me, and then went on his way. At the time I thought I would never see or communicate with him again – those were the terms he had set – but to my surprise he has reached out and I have since spoken to him on the phone a couple of times when I was passing through London.

I went back inside the room and sat for a while longer and reflected on what had just transpired. It was a surreal experience. My mind drifted as I thought about origins and destiny, and I arrived at a conclusion about myself and my own life. It wasn't a new thought, but somehow the experience of meeting my father had reaffirmed it and cemented it in my mind.

All the 'what ifs' that were buried deep inside me were brought to the surface – all the different directions that my life could have taken if he had been there, if he had been a real father to me. If he had claimed me as a baby, if he had stayed in Jamaica and brought me up, if he had taken me to England as his son, so many possibilities of what could have been…so much that could have been so different.

It was a moment of clarity, rather than a revelation: everything had happened as it did because I was fulfilling my destiny. I was exactly where I was supposed to be – in Jamaica, working for its development and advancement. Whether or not I stayed in politics, my life's work would always be tied in with Jamaica's development, in some way.

That feeling of conviction carried me for another few months as every day I woke up energized and prepared to work towards the betterment of Jamaica, whether at CaPRI, in the Senate, in the constituency of South West St Elizabeth, or in my own business.

But the vicissitudes of Jamaican politics were still very much there, and too soon they crept back into the forefront of my life. The stable routine of the Senate, CaPRI, and my other ventures that I had established was soon to be turned completely upside down by the roller coaster ride of an internal leadership challenge in the Jamaica Labour Party.

33

LEADERSHIP CHALLENGE

In September 2013, Audley Shaw announced that he was challenging Andrew Holness for the leadership of the Jamaica Labour Party (JLP). Though it wasn't until two weeks after the announcement that I publicly declared my support for Shaw, it was clear from the outset that I was in his camp. I was well aware of the formidable difficulty we would face to win.

It was no secret that some people felt that the party was not going in the right direction after its crushing election defeat in 2011. I was also concerned that we weren't moving forward, or fast enough. Almost two years had passed since the 2011 election loss and the party, in my opinion, was not sufficiently engaged in a constructive rebuilding process.

A report to review the election loss had been commissioned and completed by a group of credible persons, but the report was never released, not publicly nor internally. Even I as a deputy leader did not see the report. Issues from the report were nevertheless discussed. There were concerns among a fairly large cross section of the party that if we didn't radically change our approach, we would be hard-pressed to beat the People's National Party (PNP) in the next elections.

That concern manifested itself in the 43 per cent of the delegates who voted for Audley Shaw. Shaw clearly did not win, but 43 per cent is not a small minority, and I interpreted the result to mean that a significant proportion of party members shared the concerns that prompted the challenge.

Many senior Labourites, including Mike Henry, Delroy Chuck, Marissa Dalrymple-Philbert, Rudyard Spencer, and Daryl Vaz openly supported the challenge. We did not consider ourselves members of a 'gang'; we were concerned Labourites who wanted the party to progress.

We knew going in to the challenge that a win for Shaw would be difficult because the JLP's history does not support challenges to incumbents; neither does the PNP's. I wonder what it is about Jamaica's political development that has brought about this phenomenon. But we wanted to give Audley a platform to give a different vision and view, and even if he was unsuccessful, we felt that the challenge would strengthen the party's own internal democratic process and, in turn, buttress the attempts at restructuring the party.

Andrew Holness prevailed as leader, and as I said publicly at the time, we were prepared to accept the decision of the delegates. We were disappointed in Shaw's loss, but encouraged by how the challenge energized the entire party. We hoped that energy would translate into efforts to bring the party together and move forward more in unison.

Holness's acceptance speech on the evening of his victory suggested we were off to a good start to rebuild the party. While the body language of some of his key supporters on the platform that evening betrayed that sentiment, at the time I hoped that it was merely understandable behaviour given the heat of the moment and the uncontrollable thrill of victory.

The next day I resigned from the JLP shadow Cabinet, as I ought to have, to give the newly reaffirmed leader an opportunity to name the team that he felt enjoyed his confidence. As was to be expected, I was not named to the new shadow Cabinet that the opposition leader appointed two days later. That is par for the course in situations such as these. The shadow Cabinet is absolutely the purview of the party leader to appoint and change as he wishes. I was surprised, however, by Holness's demand that I relinquish my position as senator.

Shortly after the leadership race there was a caucus of the senators. I wasn't able to attend, but at that meeting everyone agreed to submit resignation letters, and the message was transmitted to me that I should submit one myself. At first I had indicated that I would not resign, as senators are generally appointed for the term corresponding to an administration's term in office or in opposition. While the resignation and reconstitution of a shadow Cabinet is in the normal course of actions following an internal party leadership contest, I knew that there were different norms and expectations with regard to senate appointments. Senators' appointments or removal from the Senate should not be influenced by political party rules or internal party activity, but by the Constitution.

At this point, the undated resignation letters surfaced. At the time I was appointed to the Senate by Andrew Holness in early 2012, along with six of my seven other senate colleagues, I signed an undated resignation letter, as well as another letter authorizing the opposition leader to date and submit the letter to the governor general under a certain condition.

When that letter was presented to us to be signed the understanding was that it was for a specific purpose – that should an opposition senator depart from the JLP's position on a referendum being called on the Caribbean Court of Justice (CCJ) to be made Jamaica's final appellate court, the letter would be used to ensure that the opposition's position not be compromised.

The JLP's position is, and has been for many years, that before the CCJ is made Jamaica's final court of appeal, there should be a referendum held to give all Jamaicans an opportunity to participate in the decision. Whether this decision will come to a referendum or not is still, at the time of writing, to be seen. Despite the JLP's stated position on the issue, my personal view is that as a party we need to re-examine our stance, and once I am in a position to do so, I will encourage such a debate within the party, should the issue present itself as one that we have to move on.

In addition to my surprise at being expected to resign from the Senate, I also did not anticipate that my position as deputy leader for Area Council Four would be challenged, at least not in the way that it was. While I did not expect to go uncontested in my bid for re-election as deputy leader, what transpired was out of my paradigm of acceptable political machinations.

As is standard procedure in the nomination and subsequent election of deputy leaders in the JLP, I was nominated at a party meeting on September 29, 2013, at the Manning's School in Westmoreland. Again, following the normal course of events in situations like these, I submitted my nomination form to JLP Headquarters at Belmont Road, having sent it via courier to a party official in Kingston, who hand-delivered it. The story was that there was no record of my nomination form's arrival at Belmont Road, and therefore my nomination was null and void.

I initially sought to rectify the situation and do what I could to prove that the requisite procedures had been followed and the timelines adhered to – providing waybills from the courier service, and so on.

But it soon became clear, as with the fiasco over the Senate appointment and resignation letters, that it was futile for me and for the party to continue to engage on either matter. And so I ceased my attempts to prove that I had indeed submitted my nomination form on time, and I withdrew myself from the deputy leader race. I also desisted from fighting the Senate matter in the courts, despite a great deal of pressure to do so. Arthur Williams Jr, who was also forced out of the Senate, did however pursue legal action, a decision that ultimately held important consequences for my own situation.

These actions – being forced out of the Senate and the leadership – were interpreted by many as punishment for my support for Audley Shaw in the leadership challenge. Others speculated that I was being ousted as retribution for some of the remarks I made in the course of that campaign. In particular, there was the comment I had made about wanting a leader who was not insecure, what has since been referred to as my 'afraid of bright people' statement, and which has stuck with me in the years since it was uttered.

Taken in its actual context, the point I was making was about the National Democratic Movement (NDM), in response to Holness's accusation that NDM people had come in to the JLP with the intention of 'mashing up' the party. I assumed that Holness was referring specifically to me – though of course there were others, like Mikey Stern and Daryl Vaz – when he made that statement.

The case I set out to make was that I re-entered the JLP because I felt I had something positive to contribute to Jamaica, I thought that politics was the appropriate avenue for me to make my contribution, and the NDM was no longer a suitable vehicle for the type of changes I had in mind. It had to be done via one of the two political parties, and the PNP was certainly not an option. I had been a member of the JLP before, and most of my likeminded NDM colleagues had come to the same conclusion. There was never any intention, not when I was in the NDM, and certainly not once I rejoined the JLP, to do anything akin to destroying the JLP. It was an accusation that I could not let go unanswered.

In so doing, I suggested that perhaps Holness's stance was a sign of insecurity, and made the now infamous, 'we don't want a leader who is afraid of bright people' remark. This is the nuts and bolts of political theatre in Jamaica. Politicians have always and will always cast aspersions against their rivals; it is the cut and thrust of competitive, democratic politics. When those things are said it is in the context of a publicly fought battle, and people are playing to the external audience as much as they are attempting to score real political points. In the 2006 PNP leadership race, K.D. Knight said of Portia Simpson Miller, his candidate's rival, 'the PNP needs leaders who don't have to read from a piece of paper every time they talk, who attends Cabinet meetings and understands international affairs.' These kinds of licks are all in keeping with the political theatre of any campaign. I will admit though, even I didn't expect the extent to which it would cause such a melee. It became the 'wickedest' (according to the consensus among media commentators and political analysts) comment in the entire contest. One newspaper columnist described it as 'pumping molten lava through Holness's eyes, ears and nostrils'.

After all that had transpired, it seemed that Holness wanted to strip me of any position of authority that I had in the party, and on the national stage where the party was concerned. I understood the logic behind the efforts to oust me, even if I didn't agree with the tactics objectively and of course I didn't appreciate them personally.

What was less clear is why target Arthur Williams Jr? Williams, ironically, was the person who came up with the idea that we sign undated resignation letters. Like me, he would have had no idea that the idea would come back to bite him in the way that it did.

But Arthur Williams Jr was not a party to the leadership challenge and seemed not to pose any threat to the new mandate of Holness. There was nothing that he said or did that could be construed as offensive or opposing Andrew Holness. He had worked closely with Holness in the opposition leader's office after the 2011 election in an official position as chief of staff.

Arthur Williams Jr's tenure in the JLP extended to his father Arthur Williams Sr, whose political career began when he ran for the Farmers' Party in 1949. In 1959, he ran for the JLP in South Manchester, winning and losing and winning again in the elections that followed, the last time in 1980. In 1983, when Seaga called the snap election that the PNP refused to contest, he used the opportunity to eliminate Arthur Williams Sr, along with sixteen other JLP MPs, from his slate, and in so doing he ended Williams Sr's political career.

Despite his father's unceremonious ousting, Arthur Williams Jr has been a stalwart member of the JLP. Though he was never successful at the polls, he was well respected within and outside of the party for his ability to take principled positions and rise above the political fray. He represented the best of the JLP – non-tribal, statesmanlike and even-tempered. But Jamaican political culture dictates that there must be absolute loyalty to the leader, and Arthur had failed to display that. His neutrality was not enough to insulate him from getting caught in the crossfire of the leadership skirmish. It is inherent in the Jamaican body politic and a major flaw in our political system that works – to our detriment – to discourage independent thought and keep people from fulfilling the complete breadth of their potential.

I was concerned beyond the personal implications of Holness's actions for myself and for Arthur. I feared at the time that his approach was bad for the party and the need to build the unity to mount a challenge against the PNP. In that regard, my prolonging a political fight would only further contribute to the divisiveness in the party, so I chose to retreat on the Senate matter.

In any case a fight was looking more and more futile. I was being edged out of every corner that I occupied. While I was still deputy leader, there were meetings being held in my own area council without my knowledge. Holding a position in name only is meaningless. In politics, as in life, you have to choose your battles, and I decided that – unlike earlier battles I had faced in the JLP – I was bowing out of this one.

I regret signing that undated letter of resignation. Not because it was used against me or because it forced my resignation from the Senate, but because it ran contrary to the spirit of the Jamaican Constitution. It was not the right thing to do. I generally do not hold remorse for things that happened in the past, but signing those letters represents the most significant mistake I have made in my political career thus far.

Losing my senate position and my deputy leader spot were all significant setbacks for my political career and my future in the JLP. I wasn't in the Parliament, I wasn't in the Senate, I had no position in the JLP beyond caretaker in a constituency that had rejected me. There was nothing left that could be taken away from me to indicate that I was out of favour and out of power.

Clearly this was not how I had wanted things to develop. My goal was to contribute to the reform and strengthening of the JLP, and to be a member of a JLP government when the party would next take office. I had fallen short of the first aim and the second was now out of my reach. But this is life in politics. One day you are up, the next you are down, sometimes with no warning, sometimes the signs are there. Politics is by nature unpredictable, and I can't think of any politician, even those who have reached the pinnacles of power, who have not suffered setbacks at some point.

I have never expected anything to be handed to me on a platter, and I have always known and been prepared for the jousting of the political arena. Would I like the political process to be less about interpersonal rivalries and score settling? Yes, of course, because it would free up valuable time and energy to put into the work that really needs to be done – improving our political process, advocating for policy change, and working for national development. But while we work towards that, we also have to deal with what is.

Just as I had taken a step back and evaluated the entire situation when I lost the election in 2011, once again I stopped and analysed what had happened, what I wanted, and what were my political prospects, given all that had taken place.

Would I be able to operate effectively if I stayed in the JLP? In such a marginalized position would I be able to do anything that would help take the party forward? Was I fulfilling my overarching goal to serve my country given the current situation? And, the ultimate question: did I want to continue in party politics?

I decided to stand down and stand back. I stopped fighting the efforts to marginalize me. This drew a range of reactions, from criticism to commendation, and everything in between. Regardless of what anyone thought, however, I had to do what I felt in my own mind to be best for my political career, me personally, including my family, and most importantly, for the party that I remained committed to supporting and serving whether I was in its inner circle or not.

I had no regrets about all that transpired up to that point – with the exception of having signed the senate resignation letter – even with the consequences for myself. Shaw's leadership challenge was important for the JLP's internal democracy. The party's strength depends on its own internal democratic processes. We have to work for healthy internal competition, democracy, and unity. I paid a steep price for supporting a losing candidate, but far more important than my personal situation was my obligation to the party and the larger political process.

The issue of my own personal political prospects resolved for the time being, I had to figure out what to do about the constituency of South West St Elizabeth. Given all that had transpired, it was not fair to them to remain as their candidate caretaker. I had some painful decisions to make and actions to take. My withdrawal from Jamaican party politics was nearly complete.

34

SAYING GOODBYE

South West St Elizabeth is a marginal seat for the Jamaica Labour Party (JLP) under the best of circumstances. How would the constituency fare with a representative as compromised as I was? I had lost the support of the JLP party leadership, which would weaken my ability to put myself forward as a viable candidate there. Both of the constituency's councillors supported Holness in the leadership challenge. If such high approval ratings as I had in 2011 could translate to a loss such as I had suffered, then how would I manage with a divided constituency?

This was in addition to the formidable force presented by the People's National Party (PNP), which had made it clear that it would use any means necessary to keep me from regaining that seat in a national election, as they had in 2011, when they deployed some of the party's most senior and most seasoned campaigners to work with Hugh Buchanan. I knew with a high degree of certainty that the PNP would do whatever they could to keep me out of Parliament and out of any sort of political power nationally or in the JLP if they could.

It was not a matter of expediency on my part to leave a seat that I felt I could not win, but more a matter of what was in the best interest of the JLP members and supporters in the constituency, and their prospects of having their party represent the constituency in Parliament, as well as the JLP's prospects of ever winning that seat again. These were the concerns that I had to weigh extremely carefully as I considered my way forward in the midst of the fallout between myself and the JLP's leadership in early 2014.

I concluded that it would be in the party's interest to have a candidate unaffected by the political controversies related to the leadership race, and who could unite the constituency to offer the formidable challenge necessary to return the seat to the JLP. I knew all this intellectually and rationally, but it was an extremely emotional decision to resign from the constituency chairmanship.

The leadership challenge brought many changes to my personal political situation and future, but I don't care to characterize the changes as negative or positive. Change is a constant, nowhere more so than in party politics. And who is ever to know what the medium and long-term effects of such changes are? P.J. Patterson lost his seat before, Bruce Golding, Horace Chang, Ed Bartlett, Anthony Hylton; there are others.

One loss in one election is not an indication of a failure, it is democracy at work. It is an opportunity to learn from one's experiences and mistakes in order to try to better represent a constituency the next time around. Donald Sangster left the South West St Elizabeth seat after losing it in the 1955 elections, and 12 years later was prime minister. For those who stay in the game, it is never without its ups and downs, the victories and the losses, the advances and the setbacks. Anyone actively involved in party politics has to be constantly reassessing him or herself in the context of their party, of changes at the national level, and their own personal circumstances.

And so, here I was, asking what next? After the loss of my seat, and what was essentially my complete sidelining from the party, I had a lot of questions to answer for myself, and for the many people who had supported me throughout the years. Where should I go with my political career? What of the JLP, and my role in it?

My thinking was not only about my own personal situation and my own political career. I was thinking about the JLP as a whole, as well as my place in it. Our track record of electoral success over the past 25 years was unenviable. At that point, our only valid electoral victories had been in 1980 and in 2007, and 2007 we won by a slim margin. To my mind the electoral track record alone spoke to the need for internal reform.

Yet the party's track record when it has formed the government is commendable, particularly in the areas of macroeconomic management and crime reduction, two of Jamaica's most critical weaknesses. But as a party we had not managed to translate our achievements while in office into messages that convinced the electorate to vote us back in, particularly in the 2011 campaign.

The perennial problem of the JLP harks back to the beginning of the party and its founder Alexander Bustamante, and, to be fair, to Jamaica's political culture. With all that we owe Busta, he left the party a legacy of leader-centrism, which no longer serves us well, if it ever did. The JLP's leader is expected to be all-powerful – CEO, visionary and manager all at the same time. He (there has been no she, yet) is built up as a Messiah of sorts, someone who will take the party to the 'promised land', and who will create all the policies and supervise their implementation once they get there. This legacy led to the phenomenon of Seaga and the 'one-man band', or the 'one Don'.

When one person is the be-all and end-all, the organization and the structure of the party become less relevant, as has often happened to the JLP. And, though the party may find itself a strong leader, everyone is human, and everyone has weaknesses. No individual can be expected to carry an entire political movement on his or her own.

In a well-run party the organization's structure, and other senior party officials, would compensate for the inevitable weaknesses of the party's leader – as we have seen the PNP do so effectively. But in the JLP when the leader is flawed, the entire party suffers: when the leader is damaged the party is damaged. This is what happened to Seaga and to Golding to an extent.

The immediate aftermath of the leadership challenge between Andrew Holness and Audley Shaw showed that we were still operating in this sub-optimal frame. A challenge to the leadership should not have been seen as over-ambition or disloyalty by the challenger and those who supported him.

While I accepted and respected Holness's victory in the leadership challenge, I didn't agree with his approach as to my mind it was not conducive to party unity and, ultimately, the party's prospects of regaining office. Colleagues that have a common purpose – in politics, business, indeed in any endeavour – do not have to be friends, and do not have to see eye to eye on everything, to work together for the good of their shared goals. Regardless of what transpires in an internal contest, once the contest is over, it is in the interest of the organization, for the competing parties to come together, both for show and behind the scenes.

This is not an unusual approach in politics; in fact, it is the norm, especially among successful political parties. Abraham Lincoln, one of the greatest leaders in modern history, in 1861 appointed his four closest rivals to his Cabinet, and explained that, 'We needed the strongest men of the party in the Cabinet... [t]hese were the very strongest men...I had no right to deprive the country of their services.'

US President Barack Obama put the bitter race for the Democratic presidential nomination behind him when he appointed Hillary Clinton as secretary of state in his first term, despite the horrendous things that the Clintons and their supporters said about him in the nomination race. Right here in Jamaica, in the PNP, bitter rivals have come together, joined forces, and worked for their party's common good.

But the JLP wasn't there, at least not yet.

And so I came to the moment of my resignation from South West St Elizabeth. I had fully rationalized it, and intellectualized it, and come to terms with it. But going through with it and making the announcement and conveying it to the constituents, as I did in a farewell party in January 2014, was a sad occasion for me. I knew I had made the right decision, but I was at home there, and I felt that my work for the constituency was exactly what I was supposed to be doing. I had made many bonds of friendship and collegiality in my years working in the parish, and it was strange to think of not being there, not doing the work. My goodbye to South West St Elizabeth was for the constituency's sake and for the party's sake. Personally it was difficult. It was the most sentimental I have ever felt about any political decision I have ever taken.

35

Rapprochement

In February 2015, the Supreme Court of Jamaica ruled:

(1) That the request for and procurement of pre-signed and undated letters of resignation and letters of authorization by the Leader of the Opposition from persons to be appointed or appointed as Senators to the Senate of Jamaica upon his nomination is inconsistent with the Constitution, contrary to public policy, unlawful, and is, accordingly, null and void.

(2) That the pre-signed and undated letters of resignation and letters of authorization, as well as the manner of their use to effect the resignation of Senators (the claimant, in particular) from the Senate of Jamaica, are inconsistent with the Constitution, contrary to public policy and are, accordingly, null and void.

Although I had not been party to Arthur Williams Jr's legal action, the Court's decision applied to me also. Holness made a public apology to Arthur and me, and described the situation as a regrettable one that had caused embarrassment to all involved.

The Court's decision was important for Jamaica's democracy. But I was not in a hurry to return to the Senate, and I did not take any particular joy in the ruling. I was not an active member of the Jamaica Labour Party (JLP) at the time and had largely withdrawn from publicly speaking about the party or on its behalf. I had virtually nothing to do with the party's internal operations.

Nevertheless, my heart was with the JLP, and I wanted the party to succeed. I was concerned about the effect of the ruling on the party, both internally and how it would affect the electorate's perception of the party. My having been vindicated in my initial position, that I should not be forced to resign, was a minor concern, relative to the larger issues facing the party given the court's decision. However, once it became clear that Arthur and I would have to return to the Senate, I readied myself to do so.

I made the calculation that the party and its interests are bigger than any one person, whether me or the party leader, and decided I would not only return to the Senate, I would put my all into it. My role is to continue to work for democracy regardless of any personal differences between me and anyone in the party, including the leader. In any case, by that point I had moved on from whatever had transpired between myself and Holness. This was politics; I would be foolish to take it personally. I knew my worth and I was confident in who I was and what the intentions of my actions were.

To replace Arthur and me, in November 2013, Holness had appointed Dr Nigel Clarke, one of Jamaica's brightest young businessmen, and Ruel Reid, the principal of Jamaica College, one of Jamaica's most prominent high schools, to the Senate. The court's ruling rendered their appointments null and void, as, in effect, we had never left the Senate in the first place.

I met with them after the first ruling. They were extremely gracious, and we agreed that the situation was unfortunate. They acted as servants of the people, and I commended them on their willingness to serve in the first place and accepting the appointments in the midst of the uncertainty. The JLP was fortunate to be able to call on two such able actors to advocate on the party's behalf and the people's interests in the Senate. Their contributions while they were in the Senate were worthwhile and valuable. I sincerely hoped, and I told them so, that they would remain engaged with the party. They are exactly the people that the JLP needs to continue the process of strengthening and uniting the party, and making more profound the party's policy positions. (Dr Clarke later went on to represent the constituency of North West St Andrew having won a by-election in March 2018, and was then appointed Minister of Finance and the Public Service. Ruel Reid was appointed Minister of Education, Youth and Information in the JLP Cabinet in 2016, and was endorsed as the JLP caretaker in North West St Ann in April 2018.)

By this time, well over a year had passed since the ink had dried on my estrangement from the JLP. I had been extremely busy between CaPRI, consulting, and my business ventures. But now my internal compass was pointing itself back towards representational politics. I was ready to re-engage with people and with the party, and willing to work with anyone whose ultimate goal was aligned with mine, which was to restore the JLP to a united party that was capable of winning an election, taking office, and moving Jamaica forward.

When the opportunity for rapprochement with Andrew Holness came, shortly after the senate issue had been put to rest, I cautiously welcomed it. It was not just a matter of forgiveness, or of putting the past behind me. Nor was it about being conciliatory for conciliation's sake. I had learned the lesson that maintaining the peace for peace's sake did not help the party beyond the short term when we all accepted a party leader without a contest after Golding's resignation. Rather, it was about remaining above the fray as the best, most principled, and most efficient way of moving the party and the political process forward. Practically speaking, it is a view that considers that regardless of interpersonal differences and rivalries, unity of party and unity of purpose are the most important outcomes of all that we do. And so I set about repairing my relationship with Holness, which was one of the crucial bridges that had been damaged in my separation from the JLP.

I felt compelled to return to what I have always considered the most effective way of serving the Jamaican people, through representational politics. For all its flaws, politics is still the only way to effect real change in Jamaica, and we need deep, far-reaching, and fundamental changes in Jamaica that will lead to the economic advancement and social development that we have the ability to achieve and that we deserve. I believe that the JLP, despite its weaknesses, has a legacy and a cause that are worth invigorating with new ideas and new ways of doing things, to yield different and better results, for the party and for the country.

Constitutionally, an election would be due by December 2016, and if I was going to try for a seat again, I had to make the decision then to identify a constituency, become its candidate, get to know the constituency and its needs, and for the voters to get to know me.

In May 2015, I announced that I would be seeking to represent the West Central St Catherine constituency in the next general election. I had thought that my previous forays into representational politics were unpredictable and filled with drama, but nothing could have prepared me for the tumult that was about to unfold.

36

St Catherine West Central

Representational politics as an avenue for public service is a completely different dimension from any other, whether one operates in civil society, volunteers through a church, or even serves in an official body such as the Senate. It grounds you in a way that no other means of service can. When you put yourself forward as a political representative, you answer to everyone who lives in that constituency, whether they support you or not, whether they are registered to vote or not. A member of parliament (MP) is the representative of all citizens in the government, which, for all its failings, is the most powerful body that has the most effect on people's lives. Yet, for all the responsibility that comes with the role, it is hard to be truly effective, whether your party is in power or not.

I felt that I had learned a great deal from my experience as an MP, both in terms of what I would do again, and how I would adjust my approach in areas where I felt I hadn't achieved my onjectives, or hadn't proceeded towards my goals effectively.

The West Central St Catherine seat became vacant as Dr Kenneth Baugh, who had held the seat, had announced that he would retire. The constituency had a lot of similarities to South West St Elizabeth, in that it was primarily an agricultural community, and there were high levels of poverty and basic needs to be met. I thought it was a good fit for me.

Dr Baugh is the epitome of the elder statesman. He served Jamaica through representational politics in the JLP for over three decades. Not only has he been loyal to the party and a devoted member of parliament during his times in office, he is a gentleman, and is admired by Jamaicans of all political stripes for his graciousness and the quiet dignity that he exudes.

He had been the MP for the constituency since 2002, winning with 6,948 votes to the PNP's 4,244; again in 2007, 7,321 to 5,073; and holding on in the swing against the JLP in 2011, 6,371 to 4,547. Despite these victories, West Central St Catherine could not be considered a JLP 'safe seat', as it was lost in 1997 to the PNP in Dr Baugh's first attempt to represent the JLP there. One might argue that the National Democratic Movement (NDM) contender split the JLP vote that election, but the PNP would still have pipped Dr Baugh that time around, even if the NDM votes had gone to him.

Before 1997, the seat had been held by JLP veteran Enid Bennett. She first won the seat in 1976, when it was carved out of Central St Catherine, the seat which she had won in her first election in 1967, and held on through subsequent elections until 1997. But even in 1993, her victory over the PNP candidate was close. Mrs Bennett was herself remarkable, having been the first and only woman to serve an unbroken 30 years as a parliamentarian.

Before any question of whether or not the seat was 'safe' for the JLP or not, however, I had an internal contest to win first. From the outset I knew I faced an uphill battle to even get to the point of being candidate. The odds were not in my favour.

I submitted my official application to the party to vie for the seat and become the party's caretaker-candidate in May, though it was clear those were my intentions from a few months before. We were three contenders for the position. Dr

Baugh's nephew Kent Gammon, a young lawyer who has been a JLP supporter and activist since he was a teenager, wanted to be the candidate. And so did Devon Wint, the Councillor for the Point Hill Division, and a resident and well-known figure in the constituency.

Dr Baugh endorsed Wint once it was clear that his nephew was withdrawing from the contest. Andrew Wheatley, one of the JLP deputy general secretaries, declared his hand for Wint and was deeply involved in his campaign; he took a leave of absence from his post in the party to do so.

The race got hot quickly. At one point, people in the constituency blocked the roads to protest my candidacy to be the party's representative. At another point another set of party supporters blocked the roads declaring their support for me. Things got so agitated that by July, the party officially suspended all activities relating to the selection process in the constituency.

The main contention was the voters' list for the selection, which was comprised of party workers and delegates. I felt that it was incorrectly composed. Things became tense between Dr Baugh and me, and we had some difficult moments. The internal election finally was held. Despite my efforts, but as I suspected, Wint won the contest that September, polling 211 votes to my 196.

When that news broke people must have thought, that's it, Tufton's political career is finished. He can't even get a seat to run. He tried to come back and he has failed out of the blocks. This is the end for him. And from the outside it certainly looked that way.

I saw the situation differently. I was concerned about the outcome of the selection but not resigned to that fate. There had been too many inconsistencies in the process, and I was not accepting the result. My instinct told me to press on.

In early October, I moved forward with filing my formal complaint and putting in my request that the JLP Secretariat investigate the election. My objective was that the selection would be voided and re-run with a clean voters' list, which I felt would give me the nod. This was a reach, but I was determined to go through the motions, and so I persisted. Unbeknownst to me, at the very same time, Wint's position was unravelling for reasons entirely unrelated to the selection process and to the actions I was taking to challenge the result.

The details were never made public, but there were allegations of criminal impropriety against Wint. The JLP Secretariat took the allegations seriously enough to force him to withdraw as candidate-caretaker. Horace Chang, the party's general secretary, sent out a release to that effect that took many, including me, by surprise.

By early November, it had become clear that the PNP were going to announce an election date at any moment. The JLP needed to have candidates in place and on the ground campaigning already...and so I was back in the game.

Nothing had gone how I had intended or expected. I had no idea that Wint was involved in anything that would have brought about such a drastic move by the JLP. But by that point there was no time for anyone to sit in wonder at the odd turn of events. An election was upon us and everyone had ground to cover. I literally had to get to know the constituency, meet the people and hear their thoughts about the constituency's needs, and present to them my plans and ideas for the constituency. I had already been in the area for a few months, canvassing support among party delegates and workers. Now it was time for me to meet the voters and convince them that I was worth voting for.

This was unlike my campaign in South West St Elizabeth, where I had been active in the constituency for over four years when the election was called in 2007. I had only weeks this time, and I had to make the most of it. As large as the constituency is – nearly 80 square miles – I venture that I walked every square foot of it that had a navigable footpath. I was in the constituency from morning until night almost every day. I lost 15 pounds between November and election day in February.

I was reminded of my love for politics in that intense time of campaigning. The exhilaration of seeing the potential of a people and a place, and envisioning its future and the role you could play in it. This must be what makes people like me be willing to go through so much turmoil to be a part of the process. I woke up every day excited to go to the constituency, to brainstorm with the people working with me on the campaign. I had a great team of party workers who were always full of energy and ready to go.

A high point was when Enid Bennett came out to campaign with me. She was beloved in that constituency for her long years of service there. Her presence on the ground was magical. She was such an inspiration to all of us, me and the party workers. Despite our differences, I know Dr Baugh, being the gentleman that he is, would have come out if he could have, but he was unfortunately very ill.

Our spirits were high, but I wasn't unrealistic about my prospects. Despite the support that was being shown in all the divisions, even in Wint's, I knew that there may have been lingering resentment over the selection process. I also accepted that the time was short and might not be sufficient to do the necessary groundwork, as happened in 2011.

My opponent, the PNP candidate Clinton Clarke, had run against Dr Baugh in 2011. He didn't have a high profile on the national stage, but he was deeply embedded in the constituency. He had worked in the private sector up until landing a plum job with the Jamaica Urban Transport Company (JUTC), the state-owned transportation provider for Kingston, Spanish Town, and Portmore, in 2013. I was not so much worried about him as I was about the PNP machinery that would surely roll out to back him up.

In South West St Elizabeth, there was a new and promising candidate, Floyd Green. A young, bright lawyer – he was one of three lawyers who I had called in to oversee the official count in 2011, when I lost that seat by thirteen votes – and head of the G2K; I knew he was the right person to take the seat back from the PNP. Hugh Buchanan had done little, if anything, to improve the constituency during his tenure as MP. He had barely survived an internal challenge to represent the seat, just a few months before the election; he even lost the division where his own mother was councillor. The PNP party workers in the constituency were divided amongst themselves.

Floyd was full of energy and ideas for the constituency. The PNP machinery from Old Hope Road (PNP Headquarters) was not out in force, on the ground, as they had been in 2011. On that count, the PNP miscalculated. Floyd Green, if he stays in representational politics, will be a force to be reckoned with in years to come, and his winning the seat was an important fillip to his political ascent.

I was convinced that the JLP could take back South West St Elizabeth, and that the JLP would win the election. Since 1962, the seat of South West St Elizabeth has always been won by the party that wins the election and forms the government – a classic swing seat. Most of the national polls were predicting otherwise, that the PNP would handily win. But my sense of Floyd's chances and the JLP's would prove to be correct.

I went to the constituency on a number of occasions to work with Floyd and campaign. I had no hard feelings about being back there, this time as a supporter and not as a candidate, but I sensed from many of the party workers and supporters that they felt some sort of guilt for not having done what would have been necessary for me to win the seat back in 2011. I felt no such regret and I didn't have any bitterness towards anyone there. I only wanted to do what I could to help Floyd win the seat, which I knew he could, and which he did.

37

ELECTION 2016

In Jamaica we can proudly say, despite our development challenges, despite the decades of economic stagnation, despite the unacceptable levels of poverty and unsatisfactory living conditions of far too many of our citizens, that no matter the outcome, there has always been a peaceful and uncontested transition of power after an election. This is something that few newly independent, former colonies can claim.

The 2007 election was historic because it ended an unprecedented, for Jamaica, four term, 18-year hold on office by the People's National Party (PNP). At the time, it was the closest margin of victory in a Jamaican election, with the Jamaica Labour Party (JLP) winning 32 seats to the PNP's 28, only a four-seat majority. Indeed, it was the closeness of this election that factored into the Electoral Commission of Jamaica's (ECJ) decision, in its 2010 realignment of constituency boundaries, to create three new seats and therefore have an uneven number of seats to be contested in the next election. East Central St Catherine, South Central St Catherine, and Central St James came into being, making 63 seats in the Jamaican Parliament, and precluding the possibility of a tie in any forthcoming election.

The 2011 election was historic because it was the first time in Jamaica that a party was being voted out after only one term in office. It was also a massive landslide victory for the PNP, which none of the polls predicted, though most had foreseen a PNP win. Nine seats were won by fewer than 300 votes, contributing to the fact that the margins in that election were tighter than in any previous election in Jamaica.

The 2016 election was historic in its own right, for many different reasons. The result alone, 32 to 31, cancelled out the previous 'closest margin ever' record of 2007. In fact, it is probably one of the closest victories in terms of seat count and popular vote in the world. (The JLP gained one more seat in a by-election in October 2017, bringing the parliamentary balance to 33 to 30.) The closeness of the victory aside, the 2016 election represented a critical juncture in Jamaica's democratic development, as reflected in how people voted and what it appears motivated them to vote, or not.

Within the party, as we campaigned in our respective constituencies, and as we discussed and strategized the national effort, we were aware of the changing trends and preferences of Jamaican voters. Our internal polls, and our analysis of recent research on Jamaican voters, had made clear a number of changes in the electorate's preferences and behaviour, factors that we incorporated into our campaign efforts.

When longtime PNP politician and then-government minister Bobby Pickersgill said in 2014 that most ordinary Jamaicans knew nothing about social media platform Twitter, and called those who expressed disagreement with the then-government's actions an 'articulate minority' who were politically irrelevant, he was only partially correct. The research that we relied on showed that the majority of Jamaica's youth were not interested in politics and/or were not planning to vote. However, a significant number of those who were civically engaged and politically charged were talking about politics – debating, conversing, and spreading and receiving information – via social media, mainly on Facebook and Twitter.

We thus devoted a fair portion of our efforts to engaging that articulate minority. Every JLP candidate established a Facebook page, and an Instagram and Twitter account. Some were adept at managing these modes of communication, and some hired experts to manage them on their behalf. However they did it, each candidate embraced, to one degree or another, social media and the importance of political engagement via those channels.

We were also aware of the main issues that were of concern to Jamaican citizens, both those who intended to vote and those who didn't. They were lack of trust in political representatives and the political process, a lack of confidence in the capability of political leaders to effect positive change and provide opportunities, particularly as relates to jobs and the economy, a general lack of political efficacy, and a sense that one's vote wouldn't make a difference in their own lives or the overall situation of the country.

For those who were engaged in the political process, many of them were not relying solely on political parties as sources of information that would influence their vote, but were more discerning, using the various means of communication available to them, social media primarily, to obtain information and discuss issues. Particularly among these voters there was a need to communicate informed ideas related to what they called 'real issues' – lack of economic growth and lack of job opportunities chief among them.

This gave us the blueprint for the campaign: appeal to those who are already engaged with clear plans and information related to the most important issues affecting Jamaicans, via multiple media channels, including social media; and do what we could to connect with the uncommitted and the apathetic, and carry a message that a JLP government could bring about meaningful progress and change in Jamaica. Our 10-Point Plan was clear and concise, was a central point of focus of the campaign, and it struck a chord with many voters, who could understand it and believe in it as possible and practicable.

As always, we had to contend with the fact that the PNP base is larger than the JLP's, and that the PNP controls more 'safe seats' than the JLP. Our strategy was to focus on the marginal seats, and get the uncommitted voters out.

Andrew Holness led a good campaign, staying on message and not relenting even when the attacks from the PNP became extremely personal. He and I had put our differences behind us, and we were a focused team as we campaigned and raised funds for the party. The JLP had a good slate of candidates, including many new people, in marginal seats.

Despite the majority of polls predicting a PNP victory, our own internal polls told us that we would win with a slim margin. The *Observer* newspaper released a poll conducted by Trinidad-based political scientist Derek Ramsamooj that confirmed our own findings. We had not publicized our own polls as a calculated decision. The PNP were overconfident that they would win, and we did not want to disturb their complacency.

The PNP's own failed campaign benefited us. Their candidate selection process in many constituencies alienated and disgruntled many of their own supporters. Their campaign was poorly designed and incoherent, and they did not have a clear or consistent theme or message. All of this suited the JLP well; we did not want to risk that they would believe our poll results and step up their game.

The fact that they ran such a poor campaign was, in its own way, remarkable. The PNP, up until the 2016 election, seemed to be untouchable when it came to effective election campaigns. Emblematic of their failed campaign was targeting Andrew Holness's house, a low-blow even in the Jamaican political mire; it gained them no advantage, and may even have backfired.

Their refusal to participate in the political debates, which by 2016 had come to be a fixture on the Jamaican election cycle, since they had been introduced in 2002, was a fatal misstep. Some read it as a disregard for the Jamaican voters and, by extension, the Jamaican people, that they didn't care to engage in a discussion on the issues. Others saw it as an indication that the party lacked confidence in its leader to participate satisfactorily in a debate, despite her good performance in the debate with Andrew Holness leading up to the 2011 election. By most counts, she won that debate. Mrs Simpson Miller said in an interview after the election that she didn't debate because the party didn't want her to. Whatever the reason, it was a grave mistake on their part.

Simpson Miller's lag between saying she was going to call an election and actually setting the date worked to the JLP's advantage. No one expected an election before mid-2016 at the earliest. As soon as the rumblings started in October 2015 we began to mobilize, even though it didn't appear that we would have sufficient time to prepare candidates and raise funds. The party was only just coming back together after the two unsettling years after the 2011 loss. The lag gave us precious time to pick up momentum. Many analysts and our own internal polls picked up the tide turning in our favour in just the last two weeks before the election day; some even put our win to the last couple of days before Thursday, February 25.

On election day I was in the constituency with my team. We were on the road, touching base with party workers and making sure people were getting out to vote as we had planned. At the end of the day I was in Kitson Town. The early numbers started to come in, and we were winning by margins in Polling Divisions (PDs) that we had not counted on, including PDs that the JLP had never won before. I was encouraged.

It was soon clear that I had won the seat, with a better margin than I had expected. We had done an internal poll that suggested that we would win but would have some challenges in some areas so we had doubled up our efforts in those areas. The results showed that our efforts had borne fruit.

As the results came in for the rest of the country, and the numbers started to indicate a path to a JLP win, our cautious hopefulness began to shift towards an expectation of victory. Floyd Green won his seat in South West St Elizabeth, by over 2,000 votes, an even bigger margin than when I had won in 2007. This was the swing seat. By the end of the night we were celebrating. The margin was slim – 32 to 31 – but we had won.

Winning marginally comes with its own challenges. Any party that wins an election has to focus on delivering on its commitments, but in this case, the stakes were extremely high. The close margin, and the changed dynamics of the electorate and citizenry, meant that the government would be scrutinized by a vigilant opposition and an alerted public and electorate. The same articulate minority that likely helped the JLP to win would hold the party to account unlike any government has been held accountable before.

Regardless of all these changes in Jamaican politics, Jamaican democracy and Jamaican elections, one crucial fact stands out: the voter turnout in 2016 was the lowest it has ever been, at 47.7 per cent. The notion that low voter turnout favours the PNP (based on the notion that the PNP's base support is larger than the JLP's base support, and that a low voter turnout suggests that only the parties' base support voters are coming out) was displaced by the JLP victory, another historical point.

The low turnout meant more than a turning of tides for the JLP. It is an alarming indicator that the majority of Jamaicans are either disenchanted with the political and electoral process, or even worse, completely disengaged. One must also consider that the recorded turnout is a percentage of those who are registered to vote. On the voter's list for the February 2016 election there were 1,824,410 registered voters, but it is estimated that there are 1.97 million people of voting age in Jamaica. That is over 100,000 people, at least, who could vote, but who have not even registered.

Regardless of which party wins any election in the future, or of how well whichever party has correctly read the voters to create a winning campaign, both parties will continue to fail the country if they can't, whether individually or collectively, solve this problem of voter apathy and citizens' disengagement from the political and civic process. It will not matter which party is in power, because as fewer people respect the rule of law, the role of the state, and the need for citizen engagement, the greater the disorder and the weaker our democracy. How we resolve this issue has to be a priority for the JLP and the PNP, whether in government or opposition, if we are truly interested in Jamaica's future.

38

FOR NOW...

My experience, work, insight, and training up to this point have allowed me to understand a great deal about government, politics, governance, and policy from many different perspectives. In almost everything I have done since I became socially and politically conscious as a teenager, I have had cause to think deeply about Jamaica's challenges and how they might be confronted and overcome.

I combine my experiences with my connection to and understanding of many different groups of Jamaicans and their dreams, needs, challenges, and hopes. Jamaica's developmental challenges are multilayered and often overlapping. It is hard to understand and/or change any one variable without involving many other variables. The complexity of our problems is often a barrier to resolving them.

Energy, crime, governance, the economy, the environment, our foreign policy – these are just a few things in Jamaica that need to be addressed by better policies that will propel and sustain economic and social development for all Jamaicans. While I do have ideas about many, if not all of these, based on my knowledge and experience in both government and policy research, specific policy proposals on any of these topics would be moot in a book like this.

Any policy is only effective if it is carefully constructed with full and authentic stakeholder participation, based on reliable data, and with a clear understanding of all the variables involved. Policies have to be designed on a case-by-case basis – taking best practice and research into consideration, of course – but tailored to the particular situation.

What most of us Jamaicans want is, on the surface, fairly straightforward: a country where we can move about freely, without fear of crime or violence from criminals or the state; an economy in which people have opportunities to earn good livings for themselves and their families; schools that will prepare our children to be creative and successful participants in the world; and the satisfaction that we are in a healthy, good place, literally, and figuratively. I don't think there is much debate over, say, the contents of the Vision 2030 National Development Plan picture of an ideal Jamaica. Where there is debate, and great difficulty, is in how we get there.

Regardless of whatever policy prescription is put forward, regardless of whatever ideology undergirds the vision for change and the prospects for our country's future, Jamaica can't make the changes necessary to progress unless we have a change of mindset. This change has to encompass the way we practise our politics, how we educate our children and ourselves, and how we function together as a society. Ideology may buttress the mindset change, and specific policy prescriptions may emanate from the mindset change, but first is the mindset.

First order of business is changing our political practice. We are steeped in a political culture of paternalism, tribalism, and divisiveness. While competition can be healthy in many different aspects of life, and it is at the core of a democracy, there is a point where it can be counterproductive, if not channelled in the right direction. Jamaica's political culture contains a negative manifestation of our competitive spirit.

The flip side of the overaggressive tribalism is equally if not a more serious problem: indifference. Too many people are not engaged, don't care, and don't think their vote means anything. They have divorced themselves from the system. Both attitudes – tribalism and apathy – run counter to the cooperation and healthy participation necessary for a democracy to function, flourish, and provide a framework for the country to advance.

We need to move away from the paternalistic dependency that has become ingrained in our system, to a more participatory and inclusive politics comprised of transparency, good governance, and fairness. All of the issues that are found to cause voter apathy need to be addressed. We need to focus on the quality of representation and respectful responsiveness to citizens. Other countries have grappled with and, with varying degrees of success, tackled voter indifference, especially among young people, with targeted public education campaigns, including some innovative and creative methods. Jamaica has to move in this direction.

Hand in hand with a new politics should be a reconfiguration of how we work together as a people. There is agreement among those who have studied Jamaica's development problems and compared them to countries all around the world, that Jamaica's overarching weakness is that we lack a social consensus that will take the entire country forward.

A social consensus means that everyone in the country – and those in the diaspora who remain socially, economically, and politically engaged in Jamaica – shares the same goals and the same vision. We can disagree, of course, on the means to that end, but we do not allow those disagreements to polarize us, nor do we permit class, colour, and especially not partisan lines to divide us against one another, and keep us from pursuing our objectives. It means that we each understand and agree on our own and on each others' roles and responsibilities in working towards those goals, and we agree on what rewards we are each entitled to, from our participation in the system.

And it means we agree on what sacrifices we are willing to make to achieve this.

An important aspect of a social consensus is that we are in solidarity with one another, that we all feel Jamaican and feel that being Jamaican is worthwhile in and of itself, and thus we are willing to extend ourselves not only for our own interests but for the common good. I believe that there is a basis for such solidarity in Jamaica. The fact that we all feel proud to be Jamaican when our athletes do us proud on the world stage is just one example which shows that there is a glimmer of possibility that we can unite for a common good.

Some might argue that we already have a social consensus, but that it is dysfunctional. The idea is that Jamaica's current social consensus is every man and woman for him/herself – that we are each entitled to do whatever is necessary to get ahead, regardless of rules, laws, or the consequences for others.

It is this dysfunctional consensus that has been largely responsible for our dismal economic and development trajectory up to now. How this dysfunctional social consensus came about is a result of many different factors, over a long period of time, and while it would be an interesting academic exercise to disaggregate it and identify all the different variables, I am more concerned with figuring out how to move towards something workable.

Such a transition would be an exercise that would transcend partisan politics. The full and wholehearted leadership and participation of the two major political parties, as well as any other active political parties or movements, would be a prerequisite to its success. Regardless of what we may feel about political parties, they are still, in Jamaica today and for the foreseeable future, the most important groups in any project aimed at wholesale societal change.

All non-governmental organizations, large and small, would necessarily be a part of promoting the shift from a get-what-you-can-by-any-means-necessary society to a play-by-the-rules society. The churches, the trade unions, the professional organizations, the private sector organizations, the service groups, the lodges, and the citizens' associations – any group that legitimately represents groups or sectors of the society – would have to play a part.

The participation of all these groups would comprise their endorsement of the shift to a new social consensus and of the consensus itself, and, importantly, their commitment to unrelentingly promote the consensus and its tenets in every single thing that they do, even if in doing so would preclude short term political gains. The political parties and other NGOs would be responsible for inculcating in their members the importance of the social consensus and holding their members accountable for acting in accordance with it. We all, every one of us, would have to hold the line.

Engaging Jamaicans in the name of forging a new social consensus would also bring us closer to revising our political culture. A new and functional social consensus would require that we all agree on some basic principles and goals. We would have to agree that we will all obey the rules of the society, the laws that are designed and implemented according to our democratic process. For the most part, we have good laws in Jamaica, and the design of our institutional arrangements to make and enforce laws is sound. The Westminster Model is not perfect, but we can work with it, and despite my earlier support for the National Democratic Movement's (NDM's) platform of separation of powers, I think that there are things we can do in our politics and as a people that will effect meaningful change, without an unlikely overhaul of the Constitution.

Our weakness is the lack of enforcement, which has led to a severe deficit in how we as citizens view our laws. For far too many Jamaicans, our political system and the system of institutions that govern our country are not viewed as legitimate.

The new consensus would have to comprise roles and rules that we can all, as far as possible, agree upon, about the role of societal institutions, especially the role of the government, and the role of the citizenry. We each have to view the system as legitimate, and see that we each have a stake in maintaining the system's legitimacy.

Complete consensus would be impossible, but if we are to move forward as a country and ever emerge from our economic doldrums and our problems of crime and violence, there has to be a fundamental change in the way we all do things, on an individual level and at a collective level, and that change can only come about by a deliberate movement that includes all Jamaicans.

We have had attempts at a social partnership. Social partnerships have been shown in other countries, notably Ireland, Botswana, and Barbados, to be effective mechanisms for successful policy transitions and changes. Bruce Golding in 2008 revived a process started in 2003, and established the National Partnership Council. Under the rubric 'the Partnership for Transformation', the council brought together the private sector, the unions and the government in focused discussions towards agreement on policy measures, particularly with regard to fiscal and social policy. A Partnership Code of Conduct was signed by the social partners led by Golding shortly before he resigned in 2011.

The change in administration in 2011 meant the PFT talks went on hiatus. They were revived in late 2012 by Portia Simpson Miller when she was prime minister. A secretariat, headed by Ambassador Burchell Whiteman, a widely respected (on both sides of the fence) elder PNP statesman, was established at Jamaica House. Jamaica's first ever social partnership agreement, the Partnership for Jamaica, was signed in 2013, targeting the macroeconomy, energy, doing business and the rule of law. Many credit this partnership as contributing to Jamaica's stability through the economic downturn of that period. The process continued, albeit with some name modifications, when the administration changed again in 2016. A social partnership would be an essential building block of a new social consensus, though a social consensus is broader and more far-reaching than a social partnership.

We don't need to wait on an election, or on some illusory miracle that will suddenly reverse our economic fortunes, or on the education system to be reformed, or on any single policy action or change to occur for us to start a discussion on changing our social consensus. It is a discussion and a set of actions without which Jamaica will never make meaningful and sustainable progress. This should be a priority for every single person concerned about Jamaica now and Jamaica's future, regardless of their position in society.

Talking about making such far-reaching changes raises the notion that we would need a visionary leader to motivate and mobilize. The last time Jamaica had such a leader, and such an objective for change, was Michael Manley in the 1970s. People were inspired and mobilized and change occurred; some of the changes were positive and some have left us with negative legacies that we are still grappling with. We thought we had a similar phenomenon with Bruce Golding and the NDM in the 1990s, but as it turned out, we didn't.

We don't need a charismatic leader to embark on any project, whether it is to change the social consensus or otherwise. As we saw with Michael Manley, having a visionary leader with far-reaching ideas about social and political change does not necessarily end well; indeed, in that case, many aspects ended quite badly. The Jamaican economy has never recovered from the disastrous experiments of the 1970s, though they may have been carried out with noble intentions.

It is not a once-in-a-lifetime occurrence to bring about extensive and far-reaching changes in a country's polity, and we don't have to wait on some miracle-maker to come along for us to make the changes we need to make, regardless of how far-reaching they might be.

What we need is a leader with the capacity to mobilize people towards a common goal, to explain complex ideas to just about anyone, and to be able to work with a team. What is important is a mix of policies that are carefully calibrated to meet our most important needs – poverty alleviation, economic growth, fiscal stability, a reduction in violent crime, all with an emphasis on improving social justice.

All of these areas are related to each other, and the challenge is in the details of how policies are designed and implemented so that they are positively correlated – so that improved fiscal stability results in enhanced economic growth, and so that economic growth reduces poverty and inequality.

To support, sustain and further all of this we need a radically different approach to education – the education of our children, and of ourselves. Every country in the world is grappling with how to better equip their people to successfully participate and compete in a borderless, knowledge-based economy. We in Jamaica are still lacking in how we educate our children in the basics of literacy and numeracy, and we need to continue to work on those. But we also need to be thinking about how we create critical, creative thinkers and doers and experimenters and adventurers. We need an education ethos that is framed by concepts such as joy and endeavour, collaboration and integrity, excellence and experimentation.

If we create a new generation of thinkers and innovators of this ilk they can help to take the country forward, but we need an enabling environment – a country where the rule of law is applied, where the playing field is level, where hard work is given its just reward, where a meritocracy is the norm, where we are all working toward a common goal.

To my mind, a reformed politics, including but not limited to a more internally democratic Jamaica Labour Party (JLP), is key to moving Jamaica forward in all these ways. I will be doing my part, in whatever way I can, to move this process forward, from within the JLP, and through other avenues. My allegiance is to Jamaica and the people of Jamaica, and I will serve them, one way or another.

POSTSCRIPT:
JANUARY 2019

I started working on this book shortly after the 2011 elections when I lost my parliamentary seat by 13 votes in South West St Elizabeth. At the time, I didn't anticipate that the book would take seven years to complete, nor did I have any notion of the events that would transpire between then and now.

At the outset, this book was for me a personal exercise in analysing my political career, and as circumstances began to take shape, I had in mind that the book would tell that story from beginning to end. The last chapter of the first draft, which was completed in early 2015, was my thinking through how I would contribute to national development outside of the political party system.

After the summer of 2015, I set the book aside to focus on my efforts to regain a parliamentary seat. When I returned to the manuscript in mid-2016 so much had changed and a lot of what had been written had to be revised, and new chapters added.

After the JLP's victory on February 25, 2016, and my regaining a seat in parliament, representing the constituency of West Central St Catherine, I was appointed Minister of Health by Prime Minister Andrew Holness. I was honoured to be assigned such an important ministry, humbled by the task in front of me, and grateful for the opportunity to serve in such a critical area, particularly as the portfolio affects every single citizen.

As when I was appointed Minister of Agriculture and Fisheries in 2007, I was placed in an area that I had no direct experience in. But from my perspective and based on my previous tenure, a ministerial position in a country like Jamaica is more a test of one's managerial abilities and one's ability to prioritize and mobilize resources than it is of one's knowledge of the field or lack thereof.

As soon as I learned of my appointment I began to inform myself and to surround myself with people who had expertise and experience who could advise me well. As I write this, it is two years into the JLP's administration and into my tenure in Health. In Jamaica, the critical issue in health is the burden of non-communicable diseases where seven out of ten deaths are lifestyle-related – in that they are linked to diet, physical inactivity, and not knowing one's health status. The Ministry's response is to focus on prevention in the first instance by promoting lifestyle change. At the same time, less-than-adequate funding for public health has restricted access, quality of care, and timeliness of delivery of care. With 24 public hospitals (including the semi-private University Hospital of the West Indies) and 320 health centres owned and operated by the state, and the vast majority of the population without the means to access private health care, an immediate priority is upgrading and expanding the clinics to support community primary health care, and ensuring that the hospitals are equipped to deliver high quality care to all patients, regardless of their ability to pay. Ultimately however, Jamaicans must take more responsibility for our personal health. This was the origin of the Jamaica Moves programme, which was developed and launched to encourage Jamaicans to know their health status, engage in at least half an hour of physical activity each day, and eat a healthier diet. Fifteen months in, the programme has shown signs of success manifested by the many who support parish tours, and the programme receiving the prestigious Gleaner Honour Award for 2017 in the category of Health and Wellness. Following on Jamaica Moves, the Ministry has embarked on a major public education campaign on sugary drink consumption, geared towards greater awareness of the causes and consequences of obesity. Next will be a nutrition policy for schools. In the area of structural changes, we have commenced a ten-year strategic plan for public health, a national health insurance scheme to ensure universal access, and a United Nations Office of Project Services (UNOPS) assessment of a number of hospitals with the intention of upgrading these facilities to better provide curative measures.

The challenges of public health are many; however, the impact on life and productivity makes this an important task to take on and I am humbled – and excited – to be given the opportunity to lead this charge at this time.

The great economist Alan Maynard Keynes once said, 'In order to predict the future you have to invent it.' I would never dare predict what may come. If my past 20 years in politics is anything to judge by, there will surely be many twists and turns ahead of me, though I hope that by now I have had my full share of disruptive turbulence. I will move forward towards my objectives and according to plan, understand that obstacles are inevitable, and adjust my course as necessary.

Regardless of what lies ahead, I am confident that I can, and will, face it with humility, resolve, and a positive attitude; I am well schooled in that by now. I also know that no matter the circumstances, no matter what position I find myself in, I will continue to serve Jamaica to the best of my ability.

I have set my mind to it.

CPSIA information can be obtained
at www.ICGtesting.com
Printed in the USA
FSHW021026181119